CW00457650

THE HUNNS M

The Untold Story of
Woodingdean

D. Holland.

Peter Mercer

S.B. Publications

Other books on Woodingdean.
'The Hunns Mere Pit the story of Woodingdean and Balsdean' 1993
'Woodingdean Reflections and the Millennium' 2000

**This book is dedicated to my lovely grandchildren
Scott, Brendan, Roan, Oscar and Matilda**

First published in 2010 by S. B. Publications
Tel: 01323 893498
Email: sbpublications@tiscali.co.uk
www.sbpublications.co.uk

ISBN 978-185770-362-7

Designed and Typeset by EH Graphics (01273) 515527

Contents

ACKNOWLEDGEMENTS

My very grateful thanks are due to a number of people who have encouraged me to write this third book on the history of Woodingdean despite my misgivings as to whether or not there was really enough interesting historical material to take the venture forward. After foraying into the wider history of the Parishes of Ovingdean and Rottingdean from where our village developed I firmly believed that there was sufficient unfinished historical business to take the book forward.

Without the encouragement and the input of old village friends willing to recall their memories, the writing of this book would have been a little more difficult and less interesting to read. My enormous thanks to them.

My friend, fellow-author and local historian Douglas d'Enno for inspiration and encouragement, John Davies historian of Ovingdean, Richard Coates Professor of Linguistics, School of Languages, Linguistics and Area Studies, University of the West of England, Peggy and Dick Cuthbertson, Mc Clennan (Douglas) Cuthbertson, John Munro, Lynda Wymark, Robin and Sydney Goodenough, Sam Woolgar, John Price, Elsie Stowell Raymond, Edna Stowell, Peter Longstaff-Tyrrell, Patricia Lake, Joan Brevington Henk, Gordon and Jane Morris, Valerie and Don Weller, Ivor Levett, Geoff Meads, Vanessa Attword, Derek and Thelma Dove, Colin May, Terry Keller, Dave Billings, Margaret and Colin West, John and Wendy Martin, Freda Mundon, Dee Simson, Chris Yeatman, John Homewood and Mike Simmons.

I would also like to thank the staff of the East Sussex Records Office at Lewes for their kind assistance and patience in locating historical documents, the Sussex Archaeological Society, The University of Sussex Library, The Brighton Public Library, The Woodingdean Public Library and The Rottingdean Public Library, the *Victoria County History, The Brighton and Hove Gazette,* the *Evening Argus* and *The Brighton Guardian.*

My special thanks to Douglas Holland who was very aware of this book before he passed away in 2006 and for the use of his paintings of the early views of the village. My thanks also to my wife Cynthia, daughters Virginia and Vivienne and son Ross for their patience with me over the years.

FOREWORD

When I mentioned to a friend in the village that the first recorded person living in the area of modern Woodingdean was in 1296 there was a gasp of disbelief which rapidly turned into the question 'oh yes, and where did he live'? 'Well', I replied 'not quite in the village maybe, but certainly on The Wick and after all that's a part of the village.' The interest had been sown.

Writing this book on top of the other two has been a fascinating excursion again into the past and now that we are all fans of 'Who Do You Think You Are?', 'Time Team' and 'What the Victorians Did For Us', we're used to the idea of history, especially it would seem local history, and in particular the history of the places where we grew up. Not only the places, but for the events that shaped our lives as youngsters in an era long ago that we really didn't understand.

The era for me and my sister Pat was during the war in Farm Hill lying in a Morrison shelter trying to read the 'Beano' or the 'Dandy' by a dim flickering candle screened by the blackouts over the windows whilst listening to the wail of the siren on the green opposite the Downs Hotel and counting the minutes between the 'alert' and the 'all clear': the vapour trails left by the RAF as they chased the Luftwaffe out of the skies and then later the low-flying allied bombers returning via the French coast only to reload and return to bomb Germany, how the kids cheered. I remember 'Gurmo', Pat Butler's friendly old dog, running up the middle of the unmade road, giving me a lick and running off into the distance. Sometimes he stopped on his way back to say hello to our Alsatian, Teresa, and when I stroked him he warned me not to brush the fur away from over his eyes. I also remember Mrs Ruby Jenner's little school on Warren Hill that we both attended, the penny drinks from Mrs Cox's stores and the penny ice lollies from Mrs Wellers, the flat-topped pebble-dash Co-op shop, a halfpenny bread roll or a home-made penny cream bun in Doris Keller's bakery in the parade of shops, Dennis Mann's shop where Freddie Johnson lost part of his left hand one dark evening by rubbing a detonator on their shop window which disintegrated. He wondered around for hours in a stupor covered in blood until an ambulance finally caught up with him. He still lives in the village which he loves. There were Pates the greengrocers, Mrs Larcombes, old Furgie's place, Prices, Woolgars, Mrs Newbury's fourpenny meat pies and my introduction to Smith's crisps with the little blue bag, tuppenny ice creams wrapped in paper from Slaters that when they melted the ice cream would run down and drip off your elbow, fish and chips (chips were tuppence a bag) from Fanny Palmers, the old Post Office, Robinson's for our chicken feed, Price's Garage, Mr Ridds and Mrs Chapman's Tea Shop which later became Mr Pope's 'Joys Café' named after his wife. That was all the shops. I remember "Virol", thin chocolate wafer "Slam" bars and being led to the top of Farm Hill, standing in the field to watch the red glow in the night sky of the German Blitz on London fifty miles away. I well remember the song "The White Cliffs of Dover".

In 1947 there was no transport of coal which led to shortages and rationing of 14lbs a household, so in desperation all the members of the family, one by one, went to see 'Blackie' Carter at Prices in the hope of not being recognised and getting more. The shortage of coal caused long periods of blackouts, repeated from the war with no electricity, electric fires burned for three hours a day only and there was little gas for cooking, there was no central heating in those days only stone cold beds. Then the snow came on the 23rd January, the worst for one hundred and thirty years, and cars were left abandoned over the Race Hill where the wind howled and the buses refused to go. Big Ben froze and refused to work, people went to bed wearing balaclavas to keep warm and icicles hung on the inside of our windows. There was no milk or bread for several days, pipes froze, crops froze in the ground and pneumatic drills were used to lift the parsnips, telephone lines came crashing down with the weight of ice along Warren Road and the temperature plummeted to -10C, the schools closed, then it snowed again through to the 17th March. We tobogganed in Happy Valley and got hopelessly wet and cold, what few street lamps we had were all turned off and the village closed down in darkness. The Downs Cricket Club held a Christmas Dance in the Church Hall that year to cheer people up in austerity Britain, couples danced by candlelight to music from a wind-up gramophone, I remember it - I was there as an eight-year-old "helping" my mother making sandwiches. "Life with the Lyons" on Sunday's Light programme is all so distant now. I am told that the winter of 1926 was even worse for the villagers when Samual Kitson and others organised an emergency sledge run into Brighton to get food for the village. My sister Pat recalls the Guy Fawkes bonfires on the allotments between Farm Hill and Vernon Avenue where we would all meet to watch small rockets lift into the sky from Mr Smith's milk bottles and watch Catherine wheels go round hoping they would fall off and zoom around our feet. I have fond memories of the little single-decker bus running between the Downs Hotel and my school in Rottingdean in the days when Joe or Percy the drivers would stop en route merely at the wave of a hand. The price of a fare was a penny! In 1948 Cadbury's introduced bars of Fruit and Nut Chocolate but coupons were scarce so what few there were remained on the shelf. The years rolled by and things improved during our teenage years, no longer were we deprived by food rationing; later, lovely girlfriends came on the scene! I played rugby, did athletics, enjoyed shooting at Barcombe, swam on Rottingdean beach and went on to College to work very hard. We started work, got married, began sailing, travelled the world, had children and grandchildren, retired and the rest is history. Thank goodness that I am still involved in rugby, still sail and I still see my sister and the many friends that I made along the way.

Many villagers have told me that the first book 'The Hunns Mere Pit the story of Woodingdean and Balsdean' triggered an insatiable appetite for knowledge on the history of the village, a village thought of by many as having very little history, perhaps not unlike Saltdean or Peacehaven. However, the more one burrows into the past the more one finds, often unlinked in small incomplete jig saws that set off separate chains of events finally to emerge as a complete picture.

This book is rather unlike the first two, inasmuch as the *"Hunns Mere Pit"* is a history of the village and Balsdean and some of the families that helped in their creation; the second book *"Reflections and the Millennium"* is largely contemporary history, with the history of the Community Association and many of the village organisations, including the Church of the Holy Cross from its humble beginnings as a mission hall in Falmer Road. This book, however, deals with the hidden history of the village, the bit that is generally unknown, rarely spoken of or referred to now that time has long overtaken the events. It covers the hidden history of The Wick, the creation of the New Parish, the Selbach's who owned a third of the land on which the village is built and most intriguingly how the village was formally named in July 1927.

Originally I intended to use a completely new selection of photographs but it soon became evident that there was still a considerable interest in some of the original ones, and as many people were unable to obtain the first book some of the original photographs are again included. There are now over two hundred and fifty photographs in the Holland-Mercer collection and this historically important collection is still growing. One set of the collection is held by me and the other by Peggy and Dick Cuthbertson.

The past is always with us so when embarking on this book, sit quietly and, as Michael Palin says, 'take your curiosity with you'.

Peter R Mercer MA
December 2009

PROLOGUE

Prologue from *'The Hunns Mere Pit the story of Woodingdean and Balsdean';*
1993

*......in their happy valley. Today was different, he ached from the
bitter cold, his feet were bleeding and his day's hunt had been poor,
his children would go hungry again that night. His mother and
father had suffered cruelly each winter and had told their son of
the fate of the settlement growing smaller and smaller each year.
The remains of their settlement could be seen in the grass where
the tracks met between the forest and the sea. Soon he thought the
last few remaining people would move away perhaps into the
valley, perhaps westward where the hills finished at the edge of the
sea and where the weather was warmer. He didn't know what to
do, his days were nearly ended and soon his son would make the
decision. The snow stopped and the wind fell away. He stood
silently in the middle of the track hearing strange noises and
thinking he could smell newly baked bread. He closed his eyes and
wondered of the future in thousands of years' time perhaps the
winters would be just as harsh. Weariness overtook him and he lay
down in the snow.........*

The night closed in around him and he didn't seem to be conscious of its
existence, it was impenetrable and the cold irresistible but he slept until dawn.

He gazed down at his swollen foot and the pool of black blood and remembered
the stone that gashed him. Gradually he looked out from his temporary shelter
of snow at his settlement away in the distance and slowly noticed the wind had
dropped and the sun was pouring a pale yellow light over the sea. He stood up,
frozen cold through to the marrow of his bones and limped towards his home
where the path crossed the hill in the east. The hunting was poor at this time of
the year and he had gathered little food for the family. His wife didn't know
when he would return but had looked out several times. She had even looked
out during the night and marvelled at the billions of stars, pinpricks of light that
gave the land below a faint ethereal shape. She looked at the children fast asleep
on the floor, poked the embers of the fire then returned to bed. As the sun came
up they awoke to find their father standing in the doorway. They were pleased
to see him and stumbled forward with arms outspread, his wife rising and
greeting him with a smile. His youngest child came to his side, took his hand
and tugged it possessively, he was pleased to be home and sat down by the fire
to warm himself.

He watched his wife and children prepare a meal of fish and shellfish they had
collected on the beach and wild grain left over from the warmer months. She

turned towards him and saw him looking at her in admiration and smiled, she extended her hand and smiled again when he took her hand in his. He called her 'jen' and he loved her dearly. After they had eaten he laid back on the sheepskin rugs and fell asleep. In the evening they sat in silence in the semi-darkness, the only illumination being provided by the faint glow of the fire and moonlight, each with their own thoughts as to the future.

During the night a ceaseless Arctic wind with nothing to blunt its edge for a hundred miles whipped off the sea and swept high across the hills. It rattled the roof and prowled around the interior of their home. By nightfall with not a light to be seen the settlement returned to darkness and nothing seemed out of place.

In the Spring their quality of life improved and the children spent endless hours walking the hills and the beach under the cliffs where most fun could be had. Jen worked collecting the simple food they needed and he worked with the animals, tending crops and clearing the remains of the forest which their families had been doing from the very distant past. He and the other men chipped and worked flints to make into knives, scrapers and other implements and the settlement bore testament to their art. No flint mines were necessary for flints were plentiful on the surface besides which their needs were not as great as in other larger settlements away in the west. Their homes were surrounded by the remains of flints all along the top of the hill and down into the valleys they could be seen on the surface of the ground.

One day he sat looking down through the green valley, to his Happy Valley and to a flat slab of grey sea visualizing the scene thousands of years in the future. He imagined the Bronze Age people, the Romans with their large corn fields, roads and villas, the warlike Saxons, the coming of the Normans with their stone churches, medieval farmers working the land, towns with firm roads, transport, railways and near to where he sat, a village, with churches, an orphanage, schools, public houses where people would eat and drink, estates of houses - Percy Harvey's Downs Estate, the Brighton Wick Estate, Rottingdean Gardens Estate and nearest him Falmer Gardens Estate where people would eventually make their homes alongside a new business park in Hunns Mere Way. It was blissful and enjoyable and for a moment in time he imagined himself returning to this place one day in the far distant future.

In the years that followed the grass grew over the remains of the settlement and everything disappeared except for the flint and pottery artefacts that he discarded along the way. Thousands of years later archaeologists found those flint remains at the top of Falmer Road and Dick Cuthbertson discovered many of the artefacts in his garden just below where the settlement had once been.

Flint and pottery artefacts discovered by Dick Cuthbertson in his garden and the surrounding area.

PAPA'S RULES

When I was four my brother six and baby sister two
Mamma was very ill away from home so her we never knew
Papa sold real estate books bikes and furniture as well
He raised us three as best he could as I will now tell.

Each morning we heard 'Clean your teeth wash behind your ears'
Also on Fridays to each a dose of 'Syrup of Figs' in spite of tears.

Saturday was bath night one two three!
Baby Alvilde first me next and then brother Ernie
'She gets the clean water' we always complained
But - one tank was all we had unless it rained.

At the table Papa and Ernie would often burp
Papa stopped Alvilde and me said 'Ladies don't slurp'
'Use your fork - with bread to mop up egg on your plate
Show you've finished by placing knife and fork straight'
Don't fidget girl's backs up straight' he kept repeating
'Young ladies sit still until all are finished eating.'

'Girls grow up to be ladies' is what he often told us
We quickly learned his word was law, no use to fuss
Altho' Papa and Ernie lived by a different rule
We did what we were told even if it seemed cruel.

Dear Papa how he worked to raise us to be ladies
He wanted us tall and proud not to be babies
His words come back to do what we ought
He wanted us to know what mamma would have taught.

Now Ernie? All he had to learn was 'Act like a man
Use pick axe and shovel, be nice to ladies when you can.'

Many years later when Papa died
We three talked of how he had tried
To teach us girl's ladylike ways
Ernie treated us as such the rest of his days
Now Grandchildren listen to 'Nan' 'it's not too late
Remember 'Great Grandpapa's rules' when you go out on a date'.

Elsie Stowell Raymond, California USA
Woodingdean 1924-1939

The Wick valley, over a thousand years of intermittent occupation and history.

Matilda and the curious history of "The Wick"

The expression 'I live on the Wick Estate' or 'up The Wick' was in common usage until the late 1930s as a way of differentiating between the estate and the larger Downs Estate on the eastern side of the Falmer Road. It was simplistic but important to the early settlers to be able to identify on which side of the Falmer Road they lived or should I say the Downs Road for that was its name during the early years. The area itself was generally undefined but the actual Wick Estate extended from Warren Hill eastwards to Warren Avenue, north to Drove Road in the parish of Falmer and south to Warren Road, an area previously called Norton Farm, part of the Norton Estate which lay in the hamlet of Balsdean, part of the Parish of Rottingdean. During the nineteen twenties and thirties the people living there were often called the "Wickers" by those on the Downs Estate but when Farm Hill was developed on open farmland in the 1930s new families did not consider themselves as living on the Wick Estate.

Painting of the 1923 landscape by Douglas Holland of his home in Channel View Road when aged about fourteen.

The 1838 Tithe map of Rottingdean shows Wick Farm as covering 67 acres including Warren Farm House and its garden wholly on the south of Warren Road on which is now the Lawn Memorial Park and the Nuffield Hospital. At the time, Wick Farm was owned by Stephen Martin of Rottingdean who also owned the 430-acre Woodendean Farm lying to the east of what is now Falmer Road. Thus, when people said they were living on the "Wick Estate" they should have said 'I live on Norton Farm' or better still the more regal title "Norton Estate".

To the western end of Norton Farm lies the Race Hill where five parishes meet. A small part of Race Hill was in Ovingdean parish but in 1937 a area was transferred to Whitehawk (St Cuthman's) so even less of the hill is now in Ovingdean. The name is almost certainly post-1770 when horse-racing started here. Hillview Road is an old parish boundary with the houses facing Ovingdean parish. Where the north end of Hillview Road meets Downland Road there is another boundary, this time between the Falmer parish to the north and Rottingdean and Ovingdean to the south. The Brighton Racecourse which runs from Red Hill via Race Hill to Whitehawk Hill lay across the Brighton and Ovingdean parishes. Private races were held on Whitehawk Down from 1770 or earlier but the first organised races were not until August 1783. The course has changed shape from time to time and in 1839 the course was only 470m long but by 1873 it had been extended by one mile. The loop in the north side had disappeared on the 1909 map. It had been customary to give wine annually to the Lord of the manor for the use of his land and when in 1858 wine was not given, the Race Committee were refused the use of the Ovingdean section so were compelled to alter the course from near the windmill at the top of Bear Road by turning it west and finishing it southwards to the grandstand. However, this state of affairs lasted only one year as an arrangement was made with the owner William Mabbott to pay 10 guineas a year for its use. In 1859 Charles Beard bought the Ovingdean manor estate from Mabbott and being keen on horse-racing the difficulties vanished. In 1912 the Ovingdean Estate was bought by the Brighton Corporation.

The area either side of Warren Road forms the northern end of Wick Bottom a huge valley running down to the village of Ovingdean where it joins with the Greenways/ Ovingdean valley. Aerial

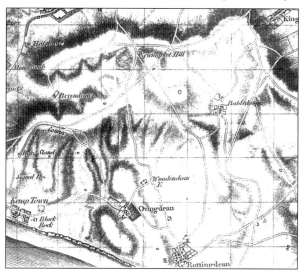

1795 showing the Wick Valley down to Woodendean.

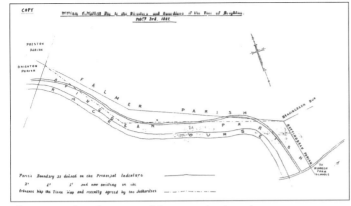

Land between the Falmer and Ovingdean Parishes bought by the Guardians of the Poor of Brighton from William Mabbott of Falmer in 1857 on which they laid Warren Farm Road to the new Warren Farm Industrial School. The path of the road followed the Race Course laid down in the middle of the 18th century.

photographs show markings at the head of Wick Bottom where there is an old-looking hedge where there may have been a settlement or large farm in the thirteenth century.

In 1901 Norton Farm was sold by Alfred Joseph Tapson and Douglas Brooke Sladen to Sir John George Blaker, the farm being 373 acres, ten acres less than had been previously measured. In March 1904 John Blaker sold off part of the farm to Alexander Luck, owner of Woodendean Farm in Ovingdean.

Rosebury Avenue in 1927 where building plots were being advertised for less than £100.

Norton Farm was heavily mortgaged over the years and passed through several owners during the decades. In 1912 the original mortgage of £6000 and interest was still due on the property. By 1919 Norton Farm was owned by Edward Leman, Harrison Simpson and George Lemen with the tithes owned by the latter. An area of the farm amounting to 13 acres, 3 roods and 3 perches was sold in the same year to Henry Pannett of Beaconsfield Road Brighton for £515 and £35 was paid to George Lemen for the tithes. Shortly afterwards, Pannett applied for planning permission to build a new estate of 96 bungalows and two new roads, Channel View Road and Seaview Road and

A young Ray Biddle and his father in Rosebury Avenue in the early 1930s. Ray took over the milk round after the War.

offered the plots for sale at £20 each. He also offered a plot with a 'brick shack' for between £100 and £200, each shack having a scullery with a bare earth floor, a kitchen/living room, sitting room, two bedrooms and a vegetable store. The estate was to be called the "Wick Estate".

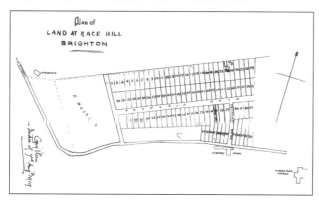

Wick Estate in 1919 showing how Henry Pannett divided the estate into 96 building plots.

Channel View Road in 1928. The road split the Wick Estate in two.

Due to the absence of piped water and electricity, also the fact that the Great War had just ended, the take up rate was slow and by 1925 the entire population of the estate consisted of only 12 families living on rough unmade roads. By 1930 the number of families had risen to 35 and the expression "I live on the Wick Estate" had been born. I believe that the Pavey family were probably the first to live here before it was known as the "Wick Estate". They lived in a bungalow built before 1895 but they were not the first recorded residents, that was a lady called Matilda some 600 years earlier.

The curious history of the "Wick" cannot be confined to the history of the small area that lays in Woodingdean, rather it is an intrinsic part of the history of both Ovingdean and Rottingdean in whose parish Woodingdean lays. The history of our village itself is therefore bound to the history of our two sister villages and it was not until 1952 that we became a new parish.

The name "Wick" is derived from the Saxon name Wic meaning a farm or settlement or possibly a dependent farm and has been in common use throughout the centuries, *viz* la Wyke 1381 Bishop Rede's register; la Wyke 1535 Valor ecclesiasticus; le Weik 1608 Survey of the Earl of Dorset's land; Le Weike 1611 rental of the Earl of

Channel View from the east end during winter.

Dorset; Weeke Bottome 1685 calendar ESRO SAS/C65/65; The Wick Bottom 1714 Grovers plan of Ovingdean; the Wick 1838 and the Wick1924. There is a Wickhovel inside Ovingdean.

The area of land around Channel View Road upon which the bungalow development took place from 1919 onwards was only a small part of the parish of Rottingdean, the principal village in the Hundred of Iwonesmere or later the Younsmere. At the time of the Domesday Survey Rottingdean, Ovingdean and Balmer were in the Welesmere Hundred while Falmer with Bevendean and Moulston (Moulsecoomb) were in the Hundred of Falmer.

There were three divisions of the Hundred of Younsmere in 1296 but the only one to be given a name was Borghemer or Balmer while the three divisions in 1326 and 1332 were Rottingdean, Ovingdean, Balsdean, Falmer and Balmer. By the end of the 16th century there were two boroughs in the Hundred, namely from Rottingdean comprehending Ovingdean and Balsdean, and Falmer. The single constable of the Hundred was chosen annually in strict rotation. Falmer paid no common fine but 4d was due annually from Rottingdean. Each married man in Rottingdean, Ovingdean and Balsdean paid two pence each half year and every bachelor who had lived there a year and a day 'and hauinge receaued the communion'a penny halfpenny. The headborough of Rottingdean, in order to make the common fine and to help repay his services, was allowed to 'pasture twenty wethers that should be freely kept for him among the flocks in Rottingdean, Balsdean and Ovingdean.' (A History of the County of Sussex Volume 7. L F Salzman: 1940).

The courts of the Hundred of Younsmere were held at the Hunns Mere Pit situated about a quarter of a mile to the brow of a hill a few yards to the left of the old road or track leading from Woodingdean to Balsdean.

Warren Avenue with Richmond Stores in the foreground in 1929. Coastal Estates Farm Hill development was still six years away from being started.

The reason for the creation of the Hundreds was simply to facilitate taxation. They were based on The Hundred Rolls, a series of land surveys undertaken across England between 1250 and 1280. Taxation is the means by which a state transfers from its subjects or citizens a part of their wealth for the support of the state and its purposes, hence the dislike and the attempt to evade payment of taxes and the ultimate tension between state and the people. Tax systems tend to decay over time as taxpayers learn to conceal their wealth, new systems are introduced and those that are based on landownership are easier to administer than those based on capital assets which can be easily hidden. Matilda it seems was the first recorded taxpayer living at the 'Wyke'.

Warren Road with the Warren Farm Dairy on the left. The cottage was the first farm building in the village. Mr Page's concrete block-making works is in the distance.

For the purpose of raising taxes the Rape of Lewes was divided into nine Hundreds, one of which was 'Hundreda of Younsmere' wherein it is recorded that in the earliest Subsidy Roll of 1296 there were eighty landowning taxpayers in Rottingdean, Ovingdean and Balmer plus a number of serfs who paid the general rate. The Rolls are the most copious single source for surnames in Sussex during the 13th century and were originally written on twenty skins of parchment, on one side of which the taxpayers of the three eastern and western rapes of the county are written in three long parallel columns arranged in the Hundreds. It is entitled in latin "The Eleventh from the county of Sussex in the 24th year of the reign of King Edward", and the endorsement runs "Eleventh of the County of Sussex". Philip de Waleby deputy of W. de Langeton, treasurer, received this Roll on the 7th day of May, in the 24th year, by the hands of Robert de Pasele, master William de Irton, the taxers and collectors of the eleventh and seventh in the county of Sussex". Robert de Pasele (of Pashly Ticehurst) who paid in the money was one of the knights of the shire in parliament at the time. The Rolls were found in 1846 among the Carlton Ride manuscripts. It lists eight or more people in Ovingdean rated at one shilling and four pence to three shillings and four pence and one person at sixteen shillings and tuppence. This latter person who had so much more land than the others was 'Matilda ate Wyke'.

Matilda relicta Hap, a widow, is also listed as a taxpayer but the exact location of her land in Rottingdean or Ovingdean is uncertain other than being in 'Villani Comitis Warrennia'. Altogether £13 9s 6d was raised in the Hundred with Matilda making the largest contribution. The personal names Matilda and Isabella were two of the more common female names the period when hereditary surnames were evolving in Sussex. The most common male name in the hundred by far was 'Will' of which there were twenty-one listed. Rob le Wadere was a pawnbroker, or one who lends on pledges and lived at Balmer, another man Will le Sopere was a soapmaker. There were, during the 14th

century, a number of instances in Sussex of persons from the class of small free tenants having hereditary surnames that appear in the subsidy roll for 1332. For instance, there were six named de Wyke at Udimore in Sussex but none in Ovingdean.

The 1296 manuscripts show that a sum of £192 2s 8d was collected on the Rape of Lewes and a total of £1449 4s 9d for all six rapes in the county. The three earliest subsidies for the county were 1296, 1327 and

The Warren Grocery Stores in the 1950s with Leslie (mounted) and Shirley Wintle shopping for ice lollies!

1332; five others followed up to 1381 thus indicating that the raising of taxes played an important but undesirable part in the lives of families living and

An earlier shot at a time when you could make a telephone call from the shop

working in Ovingdean, and in the fields and on the hillsides that eventually were to become Woodingdean. In contrast to the Younsmere the Hundreda of Walesbone covering Brystelmstone, Houve, Molescumbe, Bokkyng and Pykcumbe lists over 120 taxpayers plus serfs who contributed £39 17s 10d in taxes.

The number of taxpayers in

the later 1327 Subsidy Roll was more or less the same as the first, many being listed in the previous Rolls, but by this time Matilda ate Wyke had died or had moved away from the area which seems rather unlikely. However, Henr ate Wyke is listed in Falmer and to his credit paid 8d in tax. Another Matilda pops up as a taxpayer in 1327, Matild' ate Hyde (holding a hyde of land) is listed as living in Villata de Rottygeden and paying 6s 2d. Willmo Curtman, Rottingdean's first dressmaker is also listed. In both of the Rolls there is a rich variety of both bynames and topographical, locative, occupational and patronymic hereditary surnames many of which ramified within the county. By the 14th century there were still many families without a hereditary surname but by the 16th century names had become established. The survival of bynames and the meaning of hereditary surnames is a most intriguing and complex subject that throws a great deal of light on how people lived and worked. Civil and ecclesiastical administration was managed through the geographical and jurisdictional units of the shire, rape, Hundred and manor, and the diocese, archdeaconry, deanery and parish. All these units were in existence by about 1100 except for the parishes which gradually followed. They remained the units of administration throughout the Middle Ages.

Larcombe's General Stores in 1931 at the bottom of Vernon Avenue, the area being called the "Race Hill". The owner, Tilly Larcombe was American and lived behind the shop with her husband Edward and daughter Thelma. The shop had previously been owned by Mr Lidbetter.

By 1524 there were about eighty landowning taxpayers in the Hundred but by that time the individual contributions had risen visibly with Richard Berd (probably Beard) of Falmer paying 100s and Robert Hardman also of Falmer paying 50s. The Hardman family, apart from the Beards, were the most successful family in the area as his three brothers, Richard, John and Thomas also paid taxes.

But life in the 14th century rural economy was grim. In 1315 a mini ice age had gripped the country with long cold winters, floods and poor harvests. With no ripened corn, famine persisted along the coast with little bread to feed the people and meat too expensive to buy. The farming industry slumped, serfs starved and later in 1381 the peasants mobilised into armies and questioned the views of the landowners and the realm. In 1340 land at Rottingdean was valued at 4d per acre. In the same year it was reported that '100 Acres arable, lying annihilated by the destruction of rabbits on the land of The Earl de Warenne in Ovingdean valued at £1 5s 0d' (Blaauw 1948) which may have

Wick House and Prices Stores in the early 1930s. Both shops were part of a grand design by Vernon Chandon in 1922 for five shops and offices called the "Race Hill". Planning permission was granted but the development was never completed. After the building was demolished the tall chimney remained for many years.

been the reason for the building of a Warren Farm or coney-garth, the name used for an enclosed area for commercial rearing of rabbits. See "The Hunns Mere Pit (THMP) pages 50-52.

In the 16th century the weather had not improved. Britain was plagued by a series of mini ice ages, the Thames froze and the cold period lasted for over 200 years. We are told that in 1542 George Brownynge was the bell ringer in Ovingdean and that the roads in the village were in a pretty awful state as Thomas Barnham in his will dated 13 Oct 1544 stated *"I bequeythe to the reparyng of the hy weys yn the stret of Ovyng, ney unto the churche, wheras most ys xs."* In 1558 John Ridge, 'husbondman' and Agnes Rydge both died *'leaving their bodies to churche yeard of Ovingdean' laid side by side. John Rige (sic) 'geve to the poore men be buryed in the ther vjs viijd to be distributed for gods lowe to them at my buryall and at my monthes mynd.'* Some of the congregation looked upon the village church of St Wulfram with pride as there were several who left legacies for the 'reparacions' of the church. Perhaps the fire damage caused by French invaders in the previous century was still visible at the time. In 1549 the last of the old type of peasant's revolt to be seen in England happened, which signalled a new beginning in the type of popular uprisings. Crime was on the increase, prosecution of serious crime rose rapidly in the late 16th century reaching a peak in the late 1590s. For some, poaching or stealing became overwhelming, particularly following a poor harvest. The economy was overburdened

Vernon Chandon's dream development captured by Douglas Holland on canvas.

with financing warfare against Scotland and with such dubious governmental expedients coinage was debased. Sussex was swept by the 'English sweat', a violent form of influenza which reached epidemic proportions by the late 1550s. In the 1580s the population was worried by the threat of a Spanish landing along the south coast; by the 1590s England was involved in fighting on the high seas, in the low countries, in France and most costly of all in Ireland. The mini ice age caused by a sudden drop in sea temperature made the winters that much more unbearable and life expectancy was only forty-seven years. The fifteenth century had been a period of modest prosperity for the wage-earner, but real wages fell rapidly early in the next century, then continued to decline steadily until the 1610s when they stood at little more than one third of their 1450-75 level. Population growth produced a glut on the labour market, and those trying to sell their labour suffered accordingly. Building workers wages in the south dropped by 60% in the hundred years between 1510 and 1610. Poor law payments suggest that a pauper family of husband, wife and three children would cost £12 14s 0d to keep for a year excluding rent of £1 whilst an agricultural labourer could barely earn £15 12s 0d if he were to work every available day of the year. Higher taxation, bad harvests and the shortage of food caused severe problems at the base of society, vagrancy, poverty and popular unrest. In the mid-sixteenth century only 20% of men and 5% of women could sign their names; by 1641 adult male literacy in Sussex had risen to only 29%.

Price's Stores, part of Chandon's grand "Race Hill" scheme. The ESSO Filling Station now occupies the site.

The condition and extent of the upkeep of a parish church was once a measure of the wealth of the community, so in times of dearth the church suffered. The Chichester Diocesan Surveys of 1686-87 and 1724 were concerned with the condition of both parish and church in the late 17th and the early 18th centuries following episcopal visitations or tours of inspection and were to inform the bishop of conditions in the diocese and provide means of enforcing church discipline. Those in holy orders, together with churchwardens and sidesmen, would be subjected to examination but not other laity. The results of the first survey of Ovingdean, St.Wulfram in 1686 gives a fascinating insight into its condition *viz.*

…Church west end unpaved, seates want repair, windows decayed and the north door and door case decayed, steeple floor ruinate, bell unhung, Church and chancel want plaistering, font wholely decayed, no Commandments, no Sentences of Scriptures (on the walls), no door to the reading seat, pulpit cloath

Sam Woolgar's old butcher's shop by this time was being used by Dr Margorie and dentist Peter Southgate and Sam had moved into the three storey building on the left. Sam had a passion for sea fishing and often joined my grandfather Arthur Tolman on his boat "Redwing" out of Newhaven at a time when quality meat was difficult to buy. Taking his advice, Sam left the butchery trade to re-open in Larcombe's Stores as a wet fish shop before his new shop was ready. His son, also Sam, trained as a butcher but followed his father into the fish business. Young Sam was a popular boy in the village and now lives in Somerset.

and cushions wanting, no poor box or chest, Common Prayer Book unbound, no (book) of articals, table of degrees, nor book of Commons, no book for strangers names, Churchyard wholelly unfenced and the Parsonage house want some repairs. Chichester Diocesan Surveys 1686 and 1724: Wyn K Ford, Sussex Record Society Vol 78; Sussex Record Society, Lewes.

In comparison with the parish churches of Rottingdean, Falmer and Telscombe, St Wulfram's Church was in a greater state of disrepair, however by 1724 the Church was in much better condition as was reported, *viz.*

… the church being in tolerable order and the parsonage house and barn in good repair, four families there the biggest of them Quakers but no other dissente nor papist.

Telscombe parish church was reported as being in poor order with six families, no dissenters nor papists and Falmer church,… one wall was cracked and the thatching was required, twenty-six families, one of which Anabaptists and two Presbyterians.

St Margaret's Parish Church at Rottingdean was noted to be… in good order, Chancel in very good order also repaired by the Vicar, Sir Richard Morley having

'endowed the village with all the great tithes of the parish except those of a farm called Baseden in which there is an old chappel and chappel yard and a small parcel of land leading up to the hill belonging as it is said to the Vicar and called The Butt but never enjoyed by the present Vicar'. Vicarage house, outhouses and fences all

Richmond Stores and Tea Garden in 1928 owned at the time by Hugh and Edith Beeston, one of the first grocers to serve the Wick Estate. The shop was originally called Richmond Down Stores. The tea garden was only open in the summer.

lately new, twenty-eight families, of which one Quaker and two Presbyterian, papists none. A "butt" meaning here a shorter or irregularly shaped selion or strip of arable land in an open field, or one that abuts at right angles upon other selions. The Vicar of St Wulfram must have been rather envious of the larger community at Rottingdean but perhaps not so in 1851.

The Census of Religious Worship in March 1851 was an indication of governmental concern about the state of religion in the country and of official involvement in ecclesiastical matters. It was originally intended to question people on their religious affiliation but this was protested and it was decided to obtain information on all places of worship and their congregation. The Bishop of Oxford and the Bishop of Salisbury strongly argued that such a census would be inaccurate and open to misinterpretation (Parliamentary Debate, CXV, col 629-633), the irony being that the largest and most firmly established of the Christian bodies should be threatened. Rottingdean had its church and a Wesleyan Methodist Chapel converted from an old stable in 1839 and Falmer had, from 1800, a Particular Baptist Chapel inside a village cottage licensed as a Place of Worship by the Particular Baptists for at least fifteen years and was a branch of the Salem Baptist Chapel in Bond Street, Brighton. Services for a maximum of 50 people were held only on a Sunday evening in general. There were however no independent chapels in Ovingdean so one might expect an undivided congregation. Protestant dissent in its various forms had been narrowing the gap. The inclement weather on the day of the census coupled with a widespread influenza epidemic in the south played havoc with the results recorded. Rottingdean with a population of 1084 recorded 73 churchgoers for the morning service (6.73%) and only 77 in the evening, the Methodist Chapel which had 86 places had only 16 attending in the afternoon but an incredulous 48 in the evening. Falmer Church did better with 186 out of 573 (32.46%) with 40 attending the Baptist Chapel but the Ovingdean congregation who supported their church the most, recorded 70 parishioners present out of a population of 149 (46.90%). The three parishes lay in the registration district of Lewes with a total population at the time of 25,719 and in which there were forty Church of England and eighteen other independents including Methodists and Calvinists. There were 15,567 free places to worship in all churches and chapels, 8854 being available for the Church of England and 6713 in the chapels.

Before regular bus services began children would often play in Warren Road during the winter. The Warren Farm Industrial School is behind the flint wall built by Patching's of Brighton during the 1860s using local flints off Happy Valley and Valley Farm. The wall lasted one hundred years before being demolished for road widening.

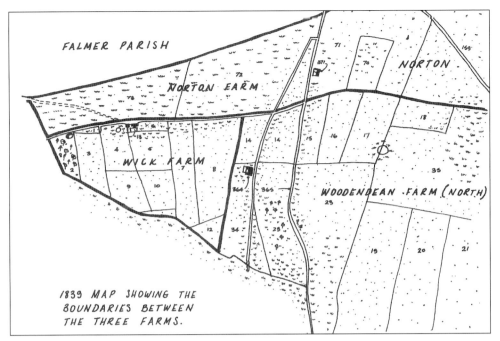

Map showing the boundaries between the three main farms, Wick, Norton and Woodendean Farm (North) in 1839.

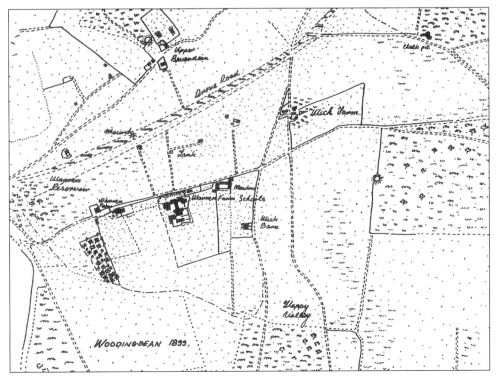

Woodingdean 1899 showing the Warren Farm and Wick Farm.

Second earliest photograph taken from Warren Hill in about 1926 and incorrectly captioned the Downs Estate. The photograph shows the Wick Estate so called from 1919 when Henry Pannett purchased the thirteen-acre site from George Luck for £515.

Postcard view in 1927 from Warren Hill. Warren Dairy Farm which succeeded Wick Farm is on the south side of Warren Road between the trees and Warren Farm Industrial School. It is said that the Dairy Farm was once an ale house selling beer to passing shepherds using the Drove Road.

Race Hill Farm, home of the Chapman family for many years until the 1950s when it was mysteriously demolished by the Brighton Corporation and the foundation stone removed to the Council's yard. See the Chapman family pages 97- 102 in THMP. Painting by Douglas Holland.

John Davies has made a particular study of the two Wick areas of Ovingdean but the western area is a particular favourite location of his and says that its 'history is mysterious and communes with nature'.

The western Wick Bottom is a steep-sided deep extension of the Greenways / Ovingdean valley that starts on the north side of Warren Road on the Norton Estate and extends south of Warren Road onto Wick Farm which was renamed Warren Farm in the 1850s, a flint-built farmhouse and barn that was sadly demolished in the 1950s for road widening. Wick Farm itself lay just outside the parish of Ovingdean. The Bottom extended southwards, down through the valley to the village of Ovingdean. A Bishop's survey of 1381-91 says *'Also in Ovyngden the tenth portion of shreaves, lambswool and cheese of la Wyke'* and is thought to be in the western Wick. The Valor Ecclesiasticus in 1535 mentions rents/tithes of 'la Wyke' in Ovingdean which must be in the eastern estate, i.e. Happy Valley. A survey of the Earl of Dorset's lands in Ovingdean refers to *"Herbag pro 8 de bovibus in & super le Weik"* which was let with other rights for £4 13s 4d yearly rent. This herbage for eight oxen on lands called "Lez Weik" is presumably around Happy Valley since the Earl never owned the manor estate. A rental book in 1611 says 'la Wyke' in Ovingdean was let by the Earl of Dorset for 13/4d per annum to Sir George Goring, Gent. This is thought to be again Happy Valley.

Warren Hill in 1929. The road was unmade at the time. Notice the carts in the garden of Henry Pavey's bungalow. Warren Hill takes its name from Warren Farm Road, the original road from Elm Grove into Woodingdean laid in 1857 to serve the School. The cost of the road was £5,269 but only able to take horses and carts.

Warren Hill in the 1930s. The first bungalow is Mrs Ruby Jenner's 'Sylvan Mount School' which many village children attended, including me and my sister. The original road into the village ran across the cultivated ground in the foreground. See 1839 map of the three original farms.

A field plan of 1714 of the eastern estate calls the land north and east of Mount Pleasant, including what we now call Happy Valley, by the name 'The Wick Bottom'. The 1839 tithe map schedules of Ovingdean and of Rottingdean show Wick Bottom as being north and east of Mount Pleasant in Happy Valley; Wick Laine as being north-west of Ovingdean Village; Wick Farm as being 67 acres north of Ovingdean parish at the Woodingdean cemetery but in the parish of Rottingdean. The schedules also show Wick Barn as being in Happy Valley and Norton Barn as being to the north of Happy Valley. The schedules contains the statement that in Balsdean there are five farms - Wick, Woodingdean, Norton, Balsdean and Bayshill-part-of Challoners.

The 1873 Ordnance Survey map shows Wick Bottom with Warren Farm where the 1839 map showed Wick Farm; it shows a new Wick Farm (in the parish of Rottingdean) at the head of Happy Valley where in 1839 there was Norton Barn. In 1928 Wick Farm, the one north of Happy Valley, is still recorded on a map and was then owned by Emma Selbach.

There is a natural division between the western and the eastern Wick Bottoms called Mount Pleasant, a 112m-high rounded hill surmounted by a triangulation station. This hill was known as 'The Round Hill' in 1714 and 1839 and as 'Mount Pleasant' by 1873, its new name probably being given by the romanticising rector Alfred Stead who lived on Cattle Hill. Along the top of Mount Pleasant runs a very ancient track dating back to Saxon or Norman times which runs through Woodingdean. It is now known as Old Parish Lane and Downsway and connects with the old drove way at the top of Falmer Road and thence on to Lewes. In 1839 this track was called Lewes Road and was privately owned by Stephen Martin of Rottingdean. In 1873 the track was divided on Long Hill, with a new branch going to Woodendean Farm. In 1896 it was decided that the original branch to Lewes was 'unnecessary for public use and that it ought not to be repaired at public expense'. Until modern times roads were often described by the places they led to. The 1714 map calls what we now know as Ovingdean Road 'The road to Lewes'; a deed of 1852 calls it 'the Woodendean Road'; an 1875 deed refers to 'the highway leading through the village of Ovingdean to the hamlet of Woodendean': and a deed of 1919 refers to it as 'main road'. Finally, the Village Hall Trust deed

A pastoral scene by Douglas Holland.

of 1932 calls it 'Woodingdean Road', as it led to Woodingdean Farm and Woodingdean Village.

In 1873 there were two dew ponds shown on the map by this path. In more modern times cricket was played on the flatter area of Mount Pleasant by the Ovingdean Cricket Club and in the late 1930s the Downs Cricket Club also played there. My father played there and my mother scored for the club. Tea was taken to the pitch on a motor bike. In 1967 a twelve-year-old boy was murdered on this path, to date his murderer has not been apprehended.

The other Wick area is on the eastern side and generally follows the Falmer Road down to Creek Valley (Long Hill) and on to the Rottingdean Valley, it is also in the Ovingdean parish. It appeared on the 1714 and 1839 maps starting at Creek Valley but by 1873 had been renamed 'Happy Valley', which is its name today. In

Warren Hill in the 1940s.

1788 it became part of the Kemp Estate when Nathaniel Kemp bought about two thirds of the eastern estate, a block of 349 acres in the middle of Ovingdean parish. When Kemp died the *'entire property had to be sold and the proceeds put in trust for his children'*. The estate was bought by Elliot Macnaghten, the recently retired chairman of the East India Company. On his death in 1888 the estate was sold to F Charsley Esq who, in 1891 started a Preparatory School in the house which lasted until 1941. In 1913 the School sold most of the estate to Alexander Luck who in turn sold the Mount Pleasant and Happy Valley area of 159 acres to the Brighton Corporation whose policy then was to maintain control over future developments. Later, the Long Hill and Creek Bottom areas

Hillview Road, the entrance to the village during the late 1930s.

were sold into private hands. Part of Happy Valley, the part which is the recreation ground was and still is in Ovingdean Parish. It was only in the previous year that the Corporation had bought the 1,041-acre manor estate of Ovingdean for £35,000 from the estate of

Steyning Beard valued at £93,030 which included much of Ovingdean, Rottingdean and Telscombe parishes. Unfortunately Beard had squandered an immense inheritance and on his death left huge gambling debts amounting to £63,000.

Farm Hill still un-adopted after the war. The author's parent's bungalow 'Iveron' arrives is furthest on the right with the bay window. The land had been previously owned by Henry Peel.

A Title Plan dated December 1929 showing the vacant land between Warren Avenue and Vernon Avenue and the proposal to build the parade of shops on Warren Road which were built later in the mid-1930s.

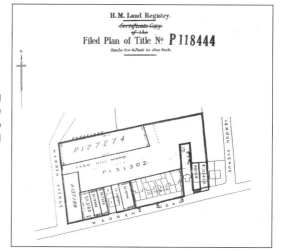

Top of Vernon Avenue in about 1950. Behind the fence on the right lay an orchard where children helped themselves!

Further up Vernon Avenue at the junction with Farm Hill in about 1950.

"Petticoat Lane", so named in a Deed made in 1922 between C H Arnold and R Noel for the sale of land in Ivor Road when Helena Road was known as Helens Road and Mc William Road was about to be laid. An Estate Office which dealt with the sale of land in this area was situated between Mc William Road and Petticoat Lane, the address of which was given as "Race Hill". After the Office was demolished Miss Clovis Warren built her holiday bungalow on the site (see THMP page 181 photograph 40). Her bungalow has recently been replaced by a modern home.

The road was renamed Downsway in about 1928 but at sometime it was called King Charles Avenue in recognition of the folklore surrounding the story that King Charles II walked down it in 1651 when an ancient track, on his journey to Ovingdean and escape to France. Downsway was part of the road linking Ovingdean with Lewes, its origins possibly going back to Saxon times. Falmer Road was previously known as 'the road from Rottingdean to Lewes' in 1714. The Church hall was completed in 1928 and the Church of the Holy Cross in 1941. For the history of the Church see WR&TM pages 18-22. This photograph was taken in the 1940s.

My sister Pat Mercer on father's motor bike in Farm Hill in 1940 with the bungalows of Vernon Avenue in the background. The area of allotments between was the only area left of the original farm owned by Harry Peel. His small farmhouse was about central between the two roads. New bungalows on Farm Hill sold in the late 1930s for £500 or £550 each.

The Wick valley has witnessed two altercations with the Brighton Councils in the last seventy-odd years, the first time was in 1938 when the Woodingdean Ratepayers Association packed a crowded Warren Farm school on 17th May of that year and in no uncertain voice told three town Councillors what they thought of their proposal to build a crematorium and cemetery in the village. The correspondent from the *Brighton and Hove Gazette* reported that he had never seen such a crowd of enthusiastic ratepayers gather together to discuss a municipal matter. Every seat, nook and corner in the school was filled and hundreds were turned away. "They shouted", he said, "they roared and booed but in spite of the fact that the good folk of Woodingdean were righteously indignant and anxious about the preposterous proposal they maintained their good humour". At the end of a very noisy evening Councillor Clout, when asked why the Corporation would not buy land outside the borough for the cemetery he replied,

" in view of the opposition to this scheme, do you expect other municipalities to jump at it?"

The Council made a full retreat to lick their wounds. However, this was not forgotten for in 1965 readers of the local newspapers would have seen one evening another headline reading "They will fight the Crematorium plan". Thirty-five people attended the quarterly meeting of the Woodingdean Community Association and unanimously resolved *"to fight to the last ditch"* a proposal to build a £116,000 crematorium beside the existing cemetery in the lawn memorial Park. *"I am utterly opposed to the crematorium being situated in Woodingdean"*, declared Councillor Fitch.

"Bleak House" in 1947 when ice covered every tree in our garden in Farm Hill.

The Association had won another battle, but perhaps not the war for in March 2010 the Argus reported on a proposal to create a new graveyard in the Warren Plantation next to an existing copse. *"Woodland burials are now popular and will be managed to benefit wild life"*, the report said.

In 2004 the Lawn Memorial Park was considered by the Brighton and Hove Archaeological Society for an archaeological investigation after aerial photographs of the area showed soil marks, possibly of ancient field systems which are thought to be of the Iron Age / Romano-British period. A number of trench excavations were made on the hillside immediately south of the cemetery and final reports on this and a resistivity survey on the nearby sheep pasture by the Society is awaited. See Brighton and Hove Archaeological Society's web site at www.brightonarch.org.uk

The parade during the 1960s before road widening.

Newmarket Farm, by Douglas Holland, at the end of Newmarket Drive overlooking the valley. To the left is Balsdean. The Latham family lived here during the 1930s. Only a few remains are still visible in the brambles.

The Selbach Saga

The Brighton Wick Estate, Brighton Heights Estate, Rottingdean Gardens Estate and Falmer Gardens Estate, Arbitration and Disillusionment.

It must be said at the very outset that no two people or developer owned more land in Woodingdean and Balsdean than the Selbachs between the two wars during which the development of the village was in its infancy. The Selbach's land holdings were nearly twice the combined area of the Downs and Wick Estates but on their land only a handful of houses in Balsdean Road had actually been built, the rest was agricultural but with enormous potential. It was the potential that Oscar Charles and Emma Daisy Sayers Selbach tried to capitalize, but in a sense failed.

The Selbach's land may be broadly split into two areas, the first comprising Balsdean, Norton and Newmarket Farms and the second area all that land lying east of the Falmer Road across to Bullock Hill which formed a natural division between the two. The first area was purely for agricultural use but the second had residential development potential. The first part, that is the three farms, was owned entirely by Oscar Charles Selbach but the second part had two owners, Emma Selbach, who owned the lions share, and Oscar Selbach who owned the rest. The overall name he gave to their holdings was the Brighton Heights Estate which encompassed the Rottingdean Gardens Estate, the lesser known Falmer Gardens Estate and the Brighton Wick Estate, the latter two being owned by Emma.

All fairly neat and simple except for one thing, Oscar desperately wanted to develop his land privately and Emma also wanted to under his direction, but certain planning restraints and covenants on the supply of water prevented the land being sold together, besides which the enforcers of a public deal to take the land into public ownership, the Brighton Corporation, were only prepared to acquire it for a rock bottom price. Oscar tried selling Emma's holdings to a London based private developer in the 1930s using a plan to build a new sanatorium and a private housing estate.

The names The Brighton Heights Estate, Brighton Wick Estate, Rottingdean Gardens Estate and the Falmer Gardens Estate are all given names by Oscar and Emma Selbach who came to Woodingdean in the 1920s from Brighton where they had been living. In 1924 they give their address as Hillcrest, Dyke Road, Brighton but by 1926 Oscar is listed as a farmer with property at Balsdean, Norton and at Newmarket Farm which Oscar bought from William Scantlebury and William Henry Percy in October 1919. By 1936 he advertised himself as a Consulting Engineer living at Wick Farm Lodge at the top of Downs Road later to be renamed Falmer Road. Three years later he was to advertise the Brighton Heights Estate Office and listed a further business called Perfection Automatic Milkers both of which were run from the Lodge.

It is not known how Emma came to hold title to her land; one line of thought is that she may have inherited it from her father, the other that she was given it on her marriage. In 1924 Oscar convinced Emma that her land had better potential if it were developed into a fashionable housing estate, to which Emma agreed and that Oscar should act as her Attorney, giving him full rein for all technical and financial matters for the development. He was given power to build and sell the houses, lay roads, sewers and services and to 'expend any money of hers' as he saw fit, but curiously she only gave him the responsibility for one year. It was a stipulation that the planned houses complied with the building bye-laws of the Newhaven Rural District Council and that no trade or business should be permitted, but this restriction should not operate to prevent the sale of poultry, fruit or vegetables or the letting of furnished apartments. All these relaxations were similar to those existing on the Downs Estate and were designed to help families after the Great War.

Some time before 1918 Oscar Selbach came to England from either America or Alaska and settled in the locality where he met and married Emma. Very little

is known of their background except that Oscar once told Edna Stowell that he was born in America but never revealed where. It is known that he had worked as an engineer in Alaska on developing the Klondike railways but at what period of his life is again not known. Whether Oscar was related to the famous American engineer Oscar Selbach, the inventor of a special racing bicycle frame, would be speculation but that Oscar did spend time in England road racing.

Oscar Selbach's own sign on a narrow Warren Road, formerly Warren Farm Road, in the early 1930s advertising the need for a Health Restoring Sanctuary in Woodingdean considered by him and his medical advisors to be the healthiest place in England.

Bill Martin and his son John with Mr Sweetman on the right in the late 1930s on Warren Way with Brighton Heights Estate in the background. The board on the left advertises a new show house being erected on the Valley Estate. Nothing is known about Sun Trap Villas except that they were to be built in Downs Valley Road, but Emma Selbach proposed to build 316 houses on this land.

Early in their married life Emma caught tuberculosis so Oscar took her to Switzerland for treatment and recuperation. He was very grateful for Emma's recovery and invited the Swiss doctors to visit England for advice on where a sanatorium should be built for the treatment of the disease. He was directed to the Downs above Brighton where he could develop his ambition. The area was described to him as being the healthiest place in England whereupon he conducted 'air tests' during the spring and autumn when the air currents were most conducive for the treatment of the disease. It is not known how long this actually took but they bought a small place at the top of Downs Road which they called Wick Farm Lodge. After they moved in Oscar turned his attention to building a sanatorium which was initially supported by the Brighton Corporation. To promote the venture Oscar erected a sign on the Race Hill advertising the fact that it was 'The Healthiest Spot in England' and 'The Health Restoring Sanctuary' and calling it 'The Brighton Heights Estate' a name seemingly unconnected with the Downs Estate which was already underway by the Downs Estate Company. His advertising boards, one on the Race Hill and the other on the crossroads directed any would be purchasers to apply for particulars at his Estates Office at the Lodge.

By 1924 Oscar had drawn up a scheme to divide the land into three hundred and sixteen plots each two hundred feet deep by forty feet wide and offer them for sale for thirty-five pounds each, much about the same price and identical in size as those on the Downs Estate. Emma is described as the vendor on an Indenture dated 13th February 1924 for the sale of plots 281 and 282 to Harold

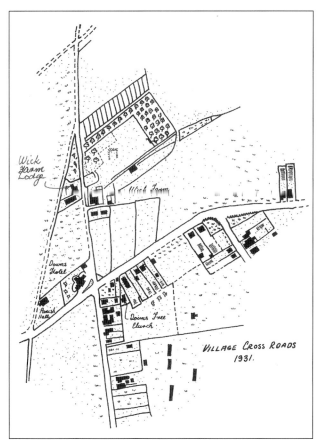

Lewin of Cawsand near Plymouth. These plots are described as being in the Parish of Rottingdean and part of The Brighton Wick Building Estate situated on a new road called Balsdean Road shown rather surprisingly as extending through to the crossroads before the name Warren Way came into being. It may be judged therefore quite fairly that it was either Oscar or Emma Selbach who gave Balsdean Road its name. Their estate was laid out with three other new roads, Wick Avenue, Seaview Row and Norton Drive each road exiting at the western end on to Downs Road. These roads of course were never built and this land was eventually used for the north Woodingdean housing estate during the mid-1950s.

Woodingdean Cross Roads in 1931. Wick Farm and Wick Farm Lodge opposite where Oscar and Emma Selbach lived are identifiable. The triangular plot of ground on the left at the top of Falmer Road was once their orchard.

Emma held the freehold title of the land and was able to convey it to purchasers in fee simple subject to the general stipulations and conditions of the Estate stated as being 'The Brighton Wick Estate'. Each plot had a building line of twenty-five feet at least on one frontage and two in cases where a road was to be laid at both ends of the property. A cost covenant stipulated that each dwelling-house should be a minimum of £400 and that no 'booth caravan, show roundabout or swing shall be permitted on any plot'. The erection of fences was mandatory and purchasers were committed to paying road and footpath maintenance until adoption by the Local Authority, the cost of which then fell to the purchaser. Fences were to be set back eight feet from the road leaving the intervening space open and unobstructed for a pavement and the planting of trees. This latter planning condition did not apply to the Downs Estate. By April 1946 there were only ten houses on the north side of Balsdean Road but none on the north side of Warren Way.

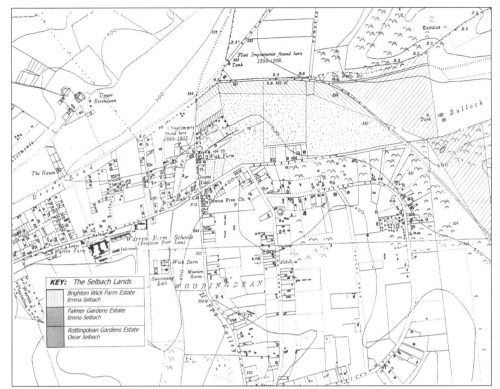

The Selbach lands split into The Brighton Wick Estate, The Falmer Gardens Estate and the Rottingdean Gardens Estate as proposed in 1937 by Oscar and Emma Selbach. The proposed sanatorium was to be sited above Wick Farm close to Falmer Road.

By the 1937 Oscar had developed his proposal for the sanatorium at the top of Falmer Road which had found favour with the Brighton Corporation but when he proposed to build a private housing estate alongside, the Corporation rejected the scheme. Oscar then proposed a better class of residential building development which would overcome the Council's objection to the proposed sanatorium scheme in itself.

Wick Barn on Mrs Emma Selbach land 'The Brighton Wick Estate.' Mr and Mrs Selbach lived opposite the barn in Wick Farm Lodge from where he sold electric milking machines under the name of 'Perfection Automatic Milkers'. In the 1950s Brighton Corporation eventually built the north Woodingdean Housing Estate on this land.

The 'Brighton Wick Estate' looking west towards the top of Falmer Road in about 1955. Oscar Selbach proposed to build his sanatorium in the foreground in the 1930s.

Bexhill Road under construction on land formerly called 'The Brighton Wick Estate'. During the 1930s Mr and Mrs Selbach proposed to develop this area of land with a high quality housing estate for the medical staff of the new sanatorium from London. Plans for the sanatorium were supported by the Town Council but not the estate. The Brighton Wick Estate finished on Norton Drive, an ancient driveway protected by law which is still there today. However, to prevent permanent future development taking place the Corporation set out to acquire the narrow area of land between what is now Bexhill Road and Norton Drive under the 'Brighton Spaces Act' of 1932. The site of a Neolithic or Stone Age settlement where, between the years 1889 and 1921, many polished axes, borers, buttons and hollow scrapers were found.

Oscar was most probably a little out of his depth by now as he turned to the backers of the sanatorium development in London in April 1937 whose Mr Gem gave personal advice and backing for the scheme. He said that *'the Brighton Town Council had not taken into account the unique curative properties of the air currents prevailing around these sites which made the property so attractive to the sanatorium people'*. He went on to say *'we feel confident the estates in question would appeal to the City men for this reason and therefore the proposal could be profitably developed as a high class housing estate'*. Mr Gem made an offer of £17,737 for 87 acres on the four estates based on renting the properties rather than selling, *viz*.

		£
13.75 acres Brighton Wick Estate East	@ £300	4125
26.25 acres Norton Top Estate	@ £250	6562
21 acres Bullock Hill, SE section	@ £150	3150
26 acres Rottingdean Gardens North	@ £150	3900
		£17,737

Naturally the offer was made subject to the plan in question being approved by the Brighton Town Council as a housing estate and that the sanatorium site be approved as a Private Sports ground and made subject to a diversion of the ancient highway known as Norton Drive. Mr Gem was keen to see the project go ahead as he finished off by saying *'the development now proposed would prove a great advertisement and asset to Brighton and eventually improve adjoining estates which would increase the revenue to the Corporation'*. Nothing then happened until March of the following year when Mr Gem urged Oscar to push his solicitors to reach an agreement with the Corporation for the sanatorium estate development to *'bring Brighton closer to the people who would enjoy living there'*.

Oscar, of course, was mindful of the risk of dealing with only one party when disposing of his very valuable land and set about seeking alternative bids from other interested parties. In August 1938 Oscar had discussions with Home Designers Ltd of London for the purchase of his Rottingdean Gardens Estate for £12,000 giving them a one month option to purchase. Later in the year he pointed out to Home Designers that the area was considered a war safety zone which would add to the value of the land. They replied they were entirely in agreement over the safety zone in time of war but hoped that it would not be necessary as a 'funk hole' but as

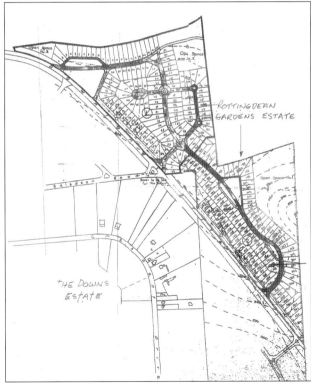

Oscar Selbach's proposed Rottingdean Gardens Estate in 1937. Several local landowners objected to the development at the time and the Brighton Corporation considered it too uneconomic to develop.

something much more beautiful and essential to mankind. Oscar was pushing them to proceed and gave them a fortnight's extension to purchase.

Oscar had at this time told Mr Gem that a further 52 acres could be made available on the Brighton Wick Estate. Mr Gem saw this as a bonus and confirmed his interest by offering Oscar £350 an acre. Oscar was juggling at this point and probably saw Home Designers' option to extend their offer by a further month as a nuisance. With so much money at stake and having to deal with the uncooperative attitude of the Brighton Corporation, Oscar called upon a Mr Smith to act as his agent. In November 1938 Mr Smith advised Oscar that he had found a definite purchaser for his Rottingdean Gardens Estate, sadly as history shows, this was not to be.

Home Designers were clearly wavering because in February 1939 they wrote to Oscar saying they needed further time to purchase Rottingdean Gardens Estate. Oscar responded by asking for evidence that the firm wished to purchase the land in question and said that he had been very ill with bronchitis and asthma following influenza and, to encourage them, said that the Brighton Corporation had scheduled their land adjoining Rottingdean Gardens on the south side for housing at a minimum build cost of £2,000. This he said proved that land in the neighbourhood was highly regarded by the Corporation. Later we shall see that when it came to the Arbitration this was not to be the case.

At this point in time Oscar could see that the negotiations for the disposal of his land into the private sector were beginning to fail and no doubt was tired and disappointed that a fortune could be gradually slipping from his grasp. The outset of the war and the tailing off of demand for new properties created uncertainties in people's minds and may have strengthened the hand of the Brighton Corporation for it was not until the war was over some six years later that Oscar finally disposed of the land at only a fraction of its pre-war potential. However, before that, things were going to get a great deal harder for Oscar and Emma.

In 1919, when Oscar purchased Balsdean, Norton and Newmarket he would not have been aware of the Brighton Corporation's intention to extend its boundaries under the Brighton Act to protect water supplies for the town. In July 1925 the Corporation bought all 793 acres of Oscar's land comprising Balsdean, Norton and Newmarket which was adjacent to the land which Oscar had been trying to sell for private residential development. These farms were sold for £14,297 10s 0d or £18 an acre in order to provide water-gathering grounds and to protect the supply, the land was then let to A W H Dalgety on an agricultural yearly tenancy for £200 a year, or 5s an acre. As part of the deal and to ensure the protection of the water supply an agreement was reached with Oscar that no pigsty, slaughterhouse, manure pit, cesspool, privy, midden or any sort of structure for the storage or disposal of sewage or effluent could be built on the lands and, for the Corporation's part, they agreed to pay a significant portion of the costs of maintaining the roads and tracks on the three farms in proportion to the Corporation's and others use. A Conveyance containing these details was drawn up between the parties as part of the Condition of Sale. Instead of Oscar holding title to the Manor of Balsdean for a long time as he may have envisaged, he was only to hold it for a few years. It must have occurred to him, however, that the effect of the restrictions and the fact that the large Balsdean Pumping Station was in full operation some little distance away would necessitate any development on his land being provided with a proper but expensive main drainage system, a point picked up later by the Corporation as part of their defence at Arbitration. The fact that a developer would not be willing to embark on such expenditure unless there was evidence of demand for housing was a key point of issue. The nearest point to Emma's land, where the main sewer was available, was 240 yards away in Falmer Road and in the case of Oscar's land 220 yards away in Crescent Drive. The cost of providing the sewer was stated as being £424 0s 0d, however, before the sewer could be laid to Oscar's land it would be necessary for land fronting the East side of Crescent Drive to be acquired or an easement agreed. The construction of cess pools was forbidden under the terms of the Conveyance.

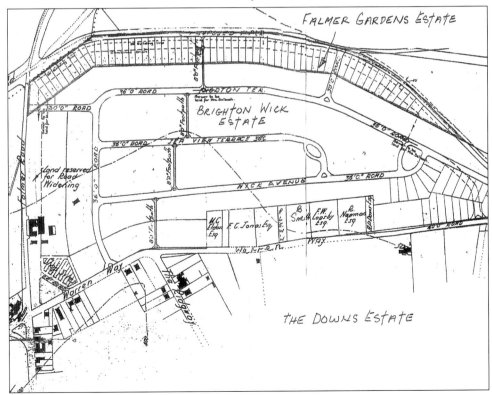

Emma Selbach's proposed Brighton Wick Estate and Falmer Gardens Estate in 1930s. Balsdean Road is incorrectly titled 'Warren Way'. Norton Drive was to have been adopted as a Town Planning Road but was rejected by the Brighton Corporation. Emma Selbach also proposed a shop development opposite the Downs Hotel.

For the development to proceed a new road on the site of Norton Drive would fall within the provisions of the covenant and therefore the cost would fall to Oscar and the Corporation in the proportion of use, but as Emma wished to develop her frontage to the new road by creating 61 building plots then it appeared to the Corporation that she should bear the whole cost.

This road was classified as a Town Planning Road but it was never built and the old Norton Drive remains today as it has been for the last thousand years.

It was early in 1937 that the Brighton Corporation made its move by refusing to grant permission for the development of Oscar's land, but after his successful Appeal to the Minister of Health, the Minister ordered that the lands could be purchased by the Corporation but only on agreed terms. Negotiations then proceeded between Oscar's surveyor Mr Warr and the Corporation, but although these negotiations were protracted no agreement was reached.

On the 18th March 1939 the two parties subscribed to an agreement which would form the basis of an Arbitration hearing for the Corporation's acquisition of a portion of Oscar's and Emma's land. The first condition of the agreement made reference to the Arbitration and 'that in the event of failure to agree the price to be paid, such price being that might be anticipated upon the assumption that the land is included in an area for which a resolution under the Town and Country Planning Act 1932 to prepare a Planning Scheme had been passed, that it was zoned in the scheme for building development for private dwelling houses and was being sold in the open market by a willing seller'. Other conditions were agreed, namely that the land was suitable for building purposes, agreement over building density, the effect of the restrictions of the Ribbon Development Act 1935 (in relation to Norton Drive), the provisions to Severance and Betterment, the conditions of the Conveyance dated 6th July 1925 in relation to the cost of main drainage, Oscar's rights to maintain and continue existing water mains under the land, there being no value attached, the joint use of the downland drive which the Corporation intended to construct in the future and finally that there was to be no provision in the agreement that water was assumed to be available. The first condition relating to the Planning Act and a development for private dwelling houses was by far the most important. The lands to be acquired by the Corporation were under two ownerships, Oscar's and Emma's.

Oscar had previously referred to his lot as the 'Rottingdean Gardens Estate' which comprised 235 building plots that lay to the east of Norton Drive, Balsdean Road and Crescent Drive and apart from a short length of frontage onto the ancient Norton Drive had no other frontage onto an existing road, lane or track. It was described as isolated downland, some distance away from the existing sparse development of Crescent Drive and in the view of the Corporation's Surveyor Haydn Nye its position, *'having due regard to the very considerable amount of available building frontage more centrally and more conveniently situated in other parts of Woodingdean I consider the possibility of its development to be remote'.*

He went on to describe the land *'as being too far distant from shops routes and other public amenities and its development uneconomic as it would not attract sufficient interest from the public to justify incurring the cost of the necessary preliminary development works. Its nearest point to the Downs Hotel is via un-made roads and is well over one thousand yards distant'.* But when Mr Nye carried out his calculations he said that *'I have not attributed a present building value to the land as ripe for development as I consider it too far distant'.*

Emma's land commenced opposite the Downs Hotel which was regarded as the pivotal centre of Woodingdean, a large area which she called the Brighton Wick Estate and according to Mr Nye, would eventually be developed. He said that *'whilst there was a certain degree of building activity in the district in the years immediately preceding the war this has been for the most part taking place on undeveloped land to the west of the Downs Hotel and Falmer Road, is very sparsely developed and there were a considerable amount of building frontages already available to made up roads'.* *'Mrs Selbach's land'* he said, *'would be slow to develop as it appeared that she would be creating further building frontages totalling some 15,430 feet or no less than 386 building plots'.*

Land upon which Emma Selbach proposed to build 61 houses called 'The Falmer Gardens Estate'.

The north Woodingdean Estate takes shape but land on Balsdean Road still lay in private hands. In 1937 only a few families lived on Balsdean Road.

However, the strip of land which the Corporation was to purchase was situated at the extreme north of Emma's land (between Bexhill Road and Norton Drive) and was the furthest from the Downs Hotel. Emma named the strip 'Falmer Gardens'. According to Mr Nye the greatest demand would be for land adjacent to Falmer Road. His valuation of the land to be acquired from Emma made provision for the eventual development over a period of ten years, that is, six plots per annum but for nine plots per annum during the first three years when preliminary advertising might invoke rather more interest in the land from potential developers.

Negotiations for the purchase of the land lasted four years and ended in stalemate and it was this that led the warring parties eventually into full Arbitration. The agreement between the two parties had expressly referred to the basis upon which the Arbitrator was to arrive at his opinion of the respective values. It was stipulated, said Mr Nye, 'that the land is to be assumed to be sold in open market by a willing seller'. As the Corporation was prima facie a willing purchaser, the compensation to be assessed is in line with the provision of section 2(ii) of the Acquisition of Land Act 1919, and no doubt this was intended. This would appear to exclude any contention by Oscar or Emma that the land had special value to the Acquiring Authority or that if such value did exist that additional compensation could be claimed in respect thereof. Mr Nye said that he had assumed that the land lay in an area where a Planning Scheme had been passed by the Local Authority under the Town and Country Act 1932. This he suggested prevented the Selbachs claiming appropriate compensation on the basis that the land was capable of development with a profit. Nye observed they agreed that the land had been zoned for development but in his view little importance could be attached to this unless it could be shown that there was a demand for the land for residential development. Under the Ribbon Development Act it would have been difficult for Oscar to develop his holding on the Rottingdean Gardens Estate and Nye was of the opinion that there would be little public interest in the building of the estate, and since there was so much more land readily available on the nearby Downs Estate then the competition would suffer, making the development impracticable, added to which there would be a very considerable cost incurred for the provision of the main services. His opinion was that no compensation would be possible and that Oscar Selbach's land was not as claimed 'ripe for development'.

So far as Emma's land was concerned the position was somewhat different inasmuch as her land enjoyed reasonable access from Falmer Road and being within easy reach of the buses and shops would attract public attention. However, the amount of her land available for building purposes was considerably more than the demand would be likely to require for some years. This was a set back for Emma.

The Ribbon Development Act which specifically required a Claimant 'to show that there is a demand for a development' necessitated proof that all 296 plots could be sold. Nye seized on this and stated that this would be very difficult to prove since the area was sparsely developed, somewhat inaccessible and a distant suburb of Brighton, besides which the Selbachs wished eventually to develop a larger number of building plots. Nye also drew attention to the Act which provided that in the case of a classified road that 'it shall not be lawful without the consent of the Highways Authority' to form or lay out any form of access to or from the road or to build any building upon the land within 220 feet from the middle of the road. Falmer Road was already by that time a classified road.

Oscar's land had no access onto the Falmer Road and his scheme relied upon the widening and improvement of Norton Drive which was no more than an unmade lane. Before anything could happen consent would have to be granted by the County Council for the lane to be used for access to the proposed building estate. In the case of Emma's land, Norton Drive was also to form the major access to the land which she would sell to the Corporation. Mr Nye thought that the Selbachs may be entitled to compensation as a result of the severance of adjacent land under their respective ownership; however, it was possible that any betterment which might accrue as a result of the undertaking, if granted to the future user of their adjoining land, be deducted from the amount of compensation paid. In the case of the claimants the area of land remaining was considerable, to Oscar 58 acres and Emma 53.74 acres and in view of the slow rate of demand and development there was sufficient land left for each of them to cater for whatever public demand there may be in years to come. Nye was convinced that no damage by severance would exist and the Selbachs were stymied.

Land upon which Oscar Selbach proposed to build 'The Rottingdean Gardens Estate'. In 1916 an enormous row broke out between politician and lawyer Sir Edward Carson MP of North End House, Rottingdean when Oscar intentionally ploughed up this land used by Sir Edward as his gallop. Selbach had little regard for Sir Edward and knew that by ploughing it up the gallop and his racing stables could be ruined. It is said that the row developed into a Court case in the following year.

Mr Nye valued Emma's land on the assumption that water could be obtained for the whole estate of 61 plots at £120 per plot less deferments over 3, 6, and 10 years which narrowed the figure to £5,924 against which he set the cost of sewers, water and gas mains and engineers' fees which reduced the value to £4,414. He then saw fit to reduce the figure again for betterment for sterilization of land, cost of access to Norton Drive, cost of obtaining water, electricity, gas, and contingencies and profit ending up with a valuation of £2416 for all 61 plots or £39 12s 1d a plot. Later on Nye was to revalue Emma's land on the basis that water could be obtained for 33 plots which revised his final valuation of the whole 61 plots to £2285.

A different principle applied to Oscar's land inasmuch as Nye thought that his land was incapable of being developed within a reasonable time due to there being no demand for houses in the area therefore its value was somewhat less, irrespective of the fact that the Corporation was prepared to give consent for housing. Craftily he inserted the suggestion that as there would be no houses built on the land it would only have an agricultural value of £30 an acre or £1,400 for all 46.7 acres.

Nye was on uncertain ground here and stated that if the Arbitrator should decide that Oscar's land had a definite building value, then his land would be worth that much more. On this assumption he valued Oscar's land made up of 235 plots at £100 per plot less an 8 year deferment which narrowed the figure to £17,178 from which he deducted the cost of roads at £11,347, a sewer connection on Crescent Drive, and the easement which further narrowed the figure after an allowance for deferments over 8 years of £9,798 to £7,380. Oscar wished to retain ownership of sixteen plots for himself so a further £519 was deducted changing the value to £6,861. Mr Nye thought long and hard on the matter and made further reductions for betterment of land, cost of water, electricity, water and gas mains, contingencies and profit and finished up with a value of £1,891 for the 216 plots or £8 15s 0d a plot.

It got worse for poor Oscar because Nye made a further valuation on the basis that water could be found for the whole development of 235 plots. His calculation for the land was made as before but he used a factor of 12 years for the development of the estate (there being no demand for housing) but commencing 2 years after. Nye arrived at the same value of £6,861 as before but after deducting the allowance for betterment, contingencies, cost of obtaining water and profit the net valuation of Oscar's land was £593 for 216 plots or £2 15s 0d a plot. However, after accounting for the cost of electricity, water and gas mains Nye stated 'that the result was likely to be a substantial deficit'.

Nye somewhat muddied the situation further by suggesting that no damage by severance would be suffered since both Oscar and Emma would retain sufficient land to enable each of them to cater for whatever public demand that there may be in years to come. Much more important was Nye's contention that the value of the land would diminish as most of the land to be acquired was situated above the 560-foot contour whilst a large part of Oscar's land was on higher ground than the Corporation's water reservoir supplying the adjacent areas, situated at the end of Balsdean Road. By virtue of Section 41 of the Corporation's Act the Corporation could not be required to provide water for building development unless the water gravitated from an existing reservoir. As most of the land that the Corporation wanted to buy was outside these limits, development on such land could not be permitted unless an express agreement was first entered into with the Corporation. Again Oscar was stymied. Although there was a water supply passing under the land the pipes were only two inch diameter and as they were considered old then any new supply could not be taken off them, beside which the mains which served Balsdean for agricultural use would be denuded. My Nye conveniently concluded that the cost of a new pumping plant would be prohibitive.

Before the Arbitration took place on the 23rd July 1946 the town Clerk J G Drew issued a confidential note to the members of the negotiating committee which summarized the situation and the compensation agreed over the years up until September 1943 and after. The note reiterated the Agreement of March 1939 in which it was agreed that the Corporation would purchase approximately 60 acres of open downland belonging to Oscar and Emma Selbach for the purpose of the Brighton No1 Planning Scheme for preservation as a public open space at a purchase price determined by arbitration. He noted that this was the culmination of a long and troublesome history regarding the land and other land belonging to Oscar Selbach who had been seeking Interim Development Permission. The previous negotiations between the Borough Engineer and Selbach's surveyor resulted in an agreement for the hypothetical development cost without the cost of constructing approach roads to the estate and the provision of services and sewers.

After extremely protracted negotiations with Nye and Donne, Solicitors, acting for Mr Selbach a settlement was made in September 1943 whereby the price for the land was agreed at £3,000 with £200 costs. This settlement was approved by the Council on the 23rd September 1943 but Oscar and Emma later denied that Nye and Donne had any authority to reach a settlement and refused to be bound by it. Then they sacked their Solicitors and recommenced negotiations with their new solicitors, Messrs Rubenstein Nash & Co.

By 1946 the value of the land from which development costs were to be deducted was set at -

Land acquired from Oscar Selbach	£4,000
Land acquired from Emma Selbach	£4,900
	£8,900

The Corporation's valuation of the new water, gas and electricity services to the sites was put forward by Mr Drew as being £8,483 12s 9d which he said would reduce the land value to a nominal £500. Rest assured Oscar did not take this lying down and argued that he could provide a water supply to the land from the bored wells at Newmarket Farm and Norton Farms under the 1925 Agreement. The Corporation repudiated this argument by saying that such an arrangement could only materialize if the Corporation and the farms' tenants agreed, which they were certainly not about to do. Oscar further argued that

John and Wendy Martin (both to the right) long-time friends of Margaret and Colin West. John came to Woodingdean in 1934 with his parents Bill and Gwendolen and after leaving Varndean Grammar School followed his father into the building industry. Bill was well known in the village which he helped to build, particularly the area around Baywood Gardens where they lived. After 73 years in the village he met and married Wendy from Burgess Hill in 2000. Margaret, nee Robinson, grew up in Robinson's Stores which opened in 1931. Margaret went to the village school followed by St Martha's Convent in Rottingdean which she did not particularly enjoy. Margaret attended Clarks College to learn secretarial work and landed a good job at Anderson and MacAuley in Brighton before entering the nursing profession at the Children's Hospital in Dyke Road. Margaret moved on to the Sussex County Hospital to qualify as a State Enrolled Nurse. After they married in the village in 1955 the couple moved to Bevendean Farm and eventually raised four children, Janet, Veronica, Bryan and Stuart who is a committed farmer. Colin's future was planned at birth. He attended Mrs Jenner's Sylvan Mount School and Varndean which he left to go on to Plumpton College in 1949-50. Colin spent his life on the farm, retiring in 2009, but has never forgotten his father's orders that he milk one cow and look after the pigs, every morning before school. With his father and brothers, Gerald and David, they built up the farm's magnificent dairy herd of 120 cows and sowed and reaped thousands of acres of cereals, potatoes, mangolds and swedes over the years. Stuart now carries on the century of downland farming started by his great-grandfather Albert West.

the cost of providing water should come from the water rates and that a water tower was unnecessary if the plant was operated on the auto-pneumatic system, and that in any case the developer's liability should not exceed £126 for providing water and finally that the cost of installing a water supply was not material to the value of the land. His argument for the cost of gas and electricity ran along similar lines, that the cost should be recouped from revenue.

It was thought that as it was unlikely that either side would depart from their positions it would mean it would be uneconomic to value the land on the basis of the agreed hypothetical development. The Corporation's surveyor Mr Nye therefore made an alternative value on the basis that part of Emma's land could be developed from existing water mains and the remainder of her land and the whole of Oscar's land as accommodation land. This resulted in a combined valuation of £3,685.

Mr Drew finished his note by saying that in 1937 the East Sussex County Council paid Oscar £7,500 for him to limit for agricultural purposes about eighty acres of land owned by him in Chailey which adjoined the land now being acquired by the Corporation, but that this price was influenced by the fact that

Selbach had secured Interim Development Permission in regard to the major part of the Chailey land and that it was not practical for the East Sussex County Council to acquire the land under compulsory powers. This agreement valued the land at £95 an acre. Oscar contended that he had an offer from a third party of £130 per acre for the land. It is interesting that this land was in fact in the Falmer Parish immediately north of Drove Road extending down into the valley towards Cambridge Farm and the dew pond on the Woodingdean - Falmer Road and in the west as far as Harold West's Bevendean Farm. See map on page 39. It is not known when Oscar Selbach purchased the eighty acres.

The 1838 Tithe map of Falmer showed most of the Parish under the ownership of Lord Chichester and William Courthope Mabbott who owned about 700 acres but let it out to William Willard, a gentleman farmer. Lord Chichester retained about twenty-five plots with houses, plantations and woodland for his own occupation including Boromer Farm which he let to George Fielder, Richard Woodman and Mr Madgwick. Lord Chichester also owned Falmer Court and a large part of 'Moulstone' which he let to William Moon. It is also interesting that in 1838 there was a cottage owned by Sarah Penfold on the north-west corner of Drove Road and Falmer Road and that there were two more cottages alongside also on the northern side of Drove Road owned and occupied by a Mr Roberts. Sarah's garden extended behind Robert's cottage on the northern side where she had a barn and a dew pond. I would think that this is a very little known fact about our village. A further cottage also owned by Mr Roberts was situated on the Drove Road just east of the roadway down into Bevendean Farm.

I do not know when the four cottages were demolished and have never seen them on any map of the area presupposing that they actually existed. In 1838 Cambridge Farm, formerly Hill Cottage, is not shown. The four cottages were just inside the parish of Falmer. In the same year Bevendean Farm is shown as having a house with half a dozen barns, the owner then being William Mabbot and the tenant William Willard. A

Harold and Peggy West celebrate their Golden Wedding Anniversary in 1981. Harold was born at the Bevendean Farm in 1902 and Peggy (real name Margaret) came from Heolgerrig in Wales. Peggy came to Brighton in 1927 to study nursing and it was whilst she was working at the Brighton General Hospital that she met Harold who she nursed through his long illness. "One day", Harold said to his doctor "I'm going to marry my nurse", and he did. See THMP Page 122 for the history of the West family.

Family of farmers. Group photograph of the West family. Back row l-r Walter, Fred and Harold, middle row, Girlie, Albert, Ellen and Laura and front row Ethel and Gertrude. The photograph is thought to have been taken in the 1940s.

small cottage and garden and two further properties known as 'Upper and Lower Croft' are also shown to the north but still within the area of the farm.

Returning to the main story of Oscar and Emma Selbach, Mr Drew then requested that the Committee inform him as to the unconditional offer that he was to make to the Selbachs on the 23rd July 1943. He did not say whether the offer was to be made before or during the Arbitration hearing which would have almost certainly been held in private away from the ears of the public and local press.During the run-up to the Arbitration hearing the Corporation compiled a document called 'Observations' the purpose of which is obscure other than to ensure some consistency and have all their experts singing off the same song sheet. In it the compiler, who almost certainly was the Town Clerk, encompassed outlines of the depositions by the experts and reiterated the historical difficulties in dealing with Mr Selbach. He also referred to the necessity of determining the price to be paid, Selbach's rights under the 1925 Agreement and finally to establish the cost of £5,028 for taking water to the land they were acquiring above the 500-foot contour well above the gravitational limit of the reservoir. Reference was again made to Oscar's successful appeal to the High Court which declared him to be at liberty to develop the land called Falmer Gardens Estate, an area of about 55 acres of the 80 acres he owned in the Chailey Rural District Council immediately north of Norton Drive. This land of course adjoined the northern section of The Wick Estate just inside Norton Drive, the limit of the

Corporation's boundary. The area of land for acquisition and preservation under the Open Spaces Act was 60 acres but at first the Selbachs would not agree to sell only the 60 acres which the Corporation wished to preserve and which comprised 12 acres of the Brighton Wick Estate belonging to Emma and 48 acres belonging to Oscar but would agree to sell as sterilised farm land only all the Norton Top, Bullock Hill and Rottingdean Gardens for a sum of £150 per acre for Emma's land and £100 per acre for Oscar's land. That amounted to £12,400. The Town Clerk said that in these circumstances the Corporation decided to include the 60 acres they wished to preserve as Public Open Space in the Town Planning Scheme and that the price be determined by Arbitration. As part of the deal the Corporation would also approve plans submitted by the Selbachs for the layout of the Brighton Wick Estate (being the remainder of the land owned by Mrs Selbach) and the Rottingdean Gardens Estate being the remaining land owned by Mr Selbach.

In March 1939 the Corporation and Oscar's surveyor Mr Warr negotiated the development costs of both new estates and arrived at a figure of £11,347 for Oscar's land and £1,405 for Emma's, however, that excluded the cost of site services and water. The Town Clerk didn't want the experts to lose sight of these development costs, and the water costs, and set them out in great detail including those provided by Mr Cathcart. He was determined that if the Corporation was to be successful at the hearing then every detail of cost be stated and plausible argument given. He reiterated a confidential discussion that he had had with Mr Whittaker of Nye and Donne regarding the provision of water to the site and that Oscar was still wishing to proceed with his developments. Whittaker wrote to the Town Clerk on the 18th November 1942 regarding the matter at hand. The Clerk replied saying that *"they would not, if they could help it, allow the development on the high land, and Council had made a fair decision in relation to their consumers and ratepayers. There was no reason whatever for the Council to incur substantial expense to the Applicants (Selbach's) land when they were determined that it not be developed."*

The matter then lay in abeyance until the summer of 1943 when Oscar's valuer made a fresh approach with an offer of £7,000 on the assumption that there was an adequate supply of water but the Town Clerk was insistent that the offer be reduced by £5,000 for the provision of the supply. This would mean that the compensation payable to Oscar would be £2,000. However, Whittaker contended that Mr Cathcart's figure was too high and that Mr and Mrs Selbach would accept £3,000 plus expenses amounting to £200. This was reported to the relative Sub Committee and at their meeting on the 7th September 1943 the Selbach's offer was accepted and agreement reached over the content of a loan of £3,250 from the Minister of Health repayable over thirty years.

All was approved and the matter settled, or so it was thought!

Five weeks later on the 18th October 1943 the Town Clerk said that he had received a letter from Mrs Selbach saying that Whittaker had no right to propose a settlement on her behalf and that the matter must be settled by Arbitration and that she was instructing new Solicitors to act on her behalf. This was backed up by Mr Selbach in writing. After this sorry state of affairs Messrs Rubenstein, Nash & Co were appointed, and according to the Town Clerk a number of meetings took place until 2nd June 1944 when a meeting was held between the Arbitrator, the Town Clerk and Mr Rubenstein when certain disclosures were made, including papers on the action against Messrs Nye and Donne for negligence which the Corporation did not object to, rather they thought that such papers might help their case, namely that the problem of water supplies were present as early as 1934. In fact it appeared that the papers did help the Corporation considerably as arguments showing up the weakness in Oscar's case voiced between him and Nye and Donne became public to the Corporation.

The Observations document contained a great deal of points made over the years that were very much against Oscar and Emma and their solicitors particularly over the question of the availability of water above the 500-foot contour. The Corporation seemed to be very unsympathetic towards Oscar in particular who was criticised heavily by sticking to the fact that he called himself an engineer and knew everything about water. This intransigence brought him into bad light when the Corporation suggested that as he professed to be an expert then he should have known that any development in such a remote place would be difficult and expensive. Oscar didn't help himself by changing to a high-powered lawyer late in the day and by his constant argument that he knew better than the Corporation's experts. For their part the Corporation were determined to acquire the land but not at any cost to the ratepayer. In the 1930s they wanted the 60 acres for Public Space which has held to this day but I dare say that it was only a few years later that they realised the potential to develop the land for public housing. This venture was most probably the catalyst they needed a few years later for taking over land under a compulsory order for the south Woodingdean Estate.

Negotiations between the Selbachs and the Corporation persisted throughout 1945 up until the 23rd July 1946 when the Arbitration was to be heard, during which time the respective experts on both sides finally agreed (without prejudice) that the price of the land was to be £4,000 for Emma's land and £4,900 for Oscar's. However, after taking into account the estimated cost of bringing to the site the various services proposed by Mr Howe, Mr Cathcart and advice from Mr Nye, their valuer, they contended that Emma's land was only worth £2,296 and Oscar's land was worthless. If they said the land was not developed then no services would be required in which case the land would be valued at £3,685 for both Emma's and Oscar's holdings.

However, a week before the hearing the Town Clerk's solicitors wrote to the Arbitrator, Mr Gillett, informing him that the Corporation had compromised the difference and that they would pay Mr Selbach £2,700 for his land and £3,300 for hers and that their costs would be referred to a Taxing Master of the High Court for apportionment. The letter also said that the Arbitration would not take place in the following week.

From that we can assume that both Oscar and Emma Selbach settled on those figures.

It was not quite the end of the story for in August 1947 the Corporation purchased a further 9 acres of land from Oscar, part of Wick Farm, under Section 2 of the Compensation (Defence) Act 1939. This small area was the ancient Wick Farm, barns and the farmyard at the top of Falmer Road, one of the oldest buildings in Woodingdean.

It was thought by some that Oscar's attempt to develop the Estate was a failure and because it fell short of its potential it caused him to become a rather disagreeable figure which in the circumstances was very understandable. Certainly his reputation in the village was that way inclined.

Oscar Selbach was a well-built man who I will always remember wearing working clothes around the village as a way of perhaps disguising his wealth which he undoubtedly had. Sam Woolgar tells me that when dressed for the occasion he was always very smart but could be rather gruff and was famed for his uncompromising attitude and would throw anyone off his land for the most trivial reason, including the Woodingdean Football Club while actually playing a game on their pitch but on his land at the top of Falmer Road. Selbach was essentially an engineer selling electric milking machines at agricultural shows rather than a builder or developer. He had few village friends but allowed Sam and Terry Keogh to build and store a fishing boat in his barn in 1950. Sam delivered meat to them, usually steak and later, when Sam's father changed to selling fish, both Oscar and Emma liked to buy the best quality turbot that money could buy. Colin May has good reason to remember Oscar because his family lived backing on to the Selbach's house and garden where he would scrump apples and lose his footballs, only to be shouted at. Colin helped his mother deliver milk from Mr West's farm and can remember his mother conversing with him but Selbach never invited them into his house. Emma Selbach was altogether a different person, she was rather charming and brought pleasure to her many village friends. Lynda Wymark who knew her well in the 1960s recalls her as being a friendly and very likeable person. On Oscar's death in the late 1950s Emma emigrated with her sister to Australia where she lived to a great age. She died in the 1990s. One person that Oscar did get on well with was Albert Stowell who arrived in the village a couple of years before Oscar and was endeavouring to make a good living by building and selling land besides acting as the local agent for the Percy Harvey Estates.

Edna Stowell, who came into the village in 1950 with her parents Mr and Mrs

Bill Sheaff who bought the garage from Harry Coe in 1950, has resided in the village for over sixty years and knew Oscar Selbach fairly well as she had had tuberculosis when the family lived in Southhampton. Oscar was interested in this fact and would often call in at the garage to talk to Edna about it. She found him a quiet private person still disillusioned by his experiences with the Brighton Corporation but Edna never got to know Emma Daisy.

It is a sad story of a devoted private couple that so few people really got to know. However sad this was for the Selbachs it was not to be the last time it occurred in Woodingdean for only a few years later in 1951 the media accused the Brighton Town Council of the "land grab" of an Ovingdean farmer's land at South Woodingdean. The farmer concerned this time was Colonel Percy Filkins whose land was valued at agricultural prices and compulsorily purchased under the Housing Act for £2,750. Only a part of his land was used for the South Woodingdean housing estate, the remaining 154 plots being sold to private developers which netted the Council £80,000. At the public enquiry experts gave evidence to the Ministry of Housing and Local Government that it was wrong that land should be compulsorily acquired and subsequently sold to private developers in order that they could carry out speculative development at a profit. The Chairman of the Housing Committee's view was that the decision to sell the land for private development was made by the Council and was approved by the Ministry of Housing, the price at which the land was sold was also approved and on each occasion the matter was made public. The principle was not a new one as the Council had sold other plots on other estates before and that they had approved similar sales since, and was based on the Government's policy to encourage the development of housing estates in a way that would bring together all classes of the community. Although a very worthy principle and well proven over the years, nevertheless Colonel Filkins was naturally incensed by being cheated out of his land so much so that he too took on the Council, not at Arbitration but in the High Court a few years later. Whereas Oscar Selbach's case was heard in private away from the eyes and ears of the village and the press, the Colonel's case made headlines that resulted in a great deal of very bad feeling towards the Council. Indeed the villagers vowed that it should never happen again in Woodingdean, but it did in 1962 when the Council's Planning Committee disagreed with the Woodingdean Community Association about what should be done with the Rudyard Road - Kipling Avenue prefab housing area. This was not so much an issue of land grabbing but one of building density and open spaces in the area. The Community Association set up a fighting fund and a campaign backed by the villagers; they employed a barrister to face the Council at a Public Hearing at which all the Council's proposals were heard in derision. In February 1964 the Association's objections were finally swept aside when the Ministry of Housing and Local Government gave the Council the go-ahead to use the land originally designated as open space for housing. This issue was not to be the last.

Bad feeling between the residents of Woodingdean and the Council simmered for many years especially when the question of land purchase occurred or when higher density building was invoked upon them. The diminishing spaces between their properties and the many new houses created ill feeling. Old landmarks disappeared, one of which was Warren House, at the top of Warren Hill, a lovely old house built in 1927 with views across the Channel owned by Mr Gardner. The property was sold in 1967 to be replaced with eight bungalows hidden as a planning requirement behind a protected screen of conifer trees.

In 1907 the first planning application was made to the Newhaven and Chailey District Council by a Mr Grimwood for the erection of a few luxury high-class houses along Warren Road that would not have disgraced Shirley Drive in Hove (See People and Places). If they had gone ahead with Mr Selbach's up-market houses on Falmer Gardens Estate alongside his sanatorium and, if the village had been granted the same protectionism as Rottingdean, then Woodingdean would have developed very differently to the way that it did. I am not suggesting that it would have been any better, but certainly different.

For more reading on Woodingdean land issues see THMP pages 76-88

◄o►◄o►◄o►

Possibly the oldest photograph of the Downs Estate. Phillip Bailey had the bungalow in the middle of the picture in 1914 and was one of the very first to live on the estate. In 1918 Harry and Alice Pitt and their three daughters took over the bungalow and erected an old army hut as a place of worship. The hut became a consecrated Mission Hall and positioned where the long poultry shed is on the left-hand side near the "road" which is barely discernible.

Wonderful view of Downs Road in the late 1920s after the Downs Hotel was opened in September 1925.

Percy Harvey and his Downs Estate

'Downs', from Old English 'Dun', a hill. 'The Downs Estate' was conceived just before the Great War by a London firm of developers, Percy Harvey Estates Ltd, who laid out the estate to occupy as much as possible the area of the Woodendean Farm except for the southern end which eventually was to become the south Woodingdean estate, hence its shape. (See 'The Brighton Downs Estate' advertising pamphlet and the 'Plan of Second Portion 1920'.)

According to John Davies, Woodendean Farm has varied in size *viz:* 1838 Rottingdean Tithe Map Schedule 430 acres, 1851 census 437 acres, 1871 census 424 acres and the Funnell measurement 392 acres. The area remained intact and within the parish of Rottingdean until 1952 when 23 acres were transferred by the Church of England to the Ovingdean parish. The area included the farm buildings and 19 acres of the former Woodendean Farm and a mansion called Woodingdean House with its grounds of 2 acres. The whole of the area is what

A view along the Downs Road in the mid-1920s. The Pitts bungalow can be seen near to the top of the photograph and the Mission Hall in the form of a long hut near the road. The flint pits in Happy Valley and in the little-known Valley Farm on the eastern side of the road can still be seen. The flints were mined by hand and taken by handcart to the Brighton Corporation yard to be used in road building. Happy Valley was probably a Bronze Age settlement for, in 1905, a flint digger discovered a bronze pin and a figure of a hog. He also discovered two saucer-size bronze discs, all about 3 feet below the surface, (Ref. Proceedings of the Society of Antiquaries of London 1906 and 1907. Second Series Vol. XXI.)

Happy Valley and Downs Road under the snow in the late 1920s. In 1714 the track was simply known "as the road from Rottingdean to Lewes", in 1810 it was called Happy Valley Road and in 1822 was opened as a coach road between Rottingdean and Lewes. Before 1920 it was called Downs Road and in the 1930s finally called Falmer Road. During the 1920s the Rottingdean end of the road was sometimes called the Woodingdean Road.

Probably taken in the harsh winter of 1926 when the village was cut off and men mounted a mercy mission to Brighton with sledges to obtain groceries for the elderly.

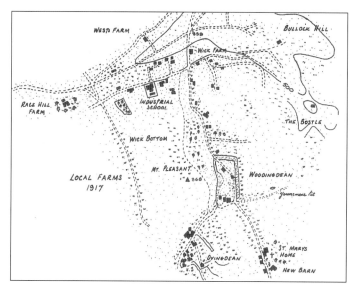

Woodingdean in 1917 showing the local farms and the first roads on the Downs Estate.

A 1927 view of the Downs Estate showing Crescent Drive and Happy Valley. where shallow flint pits are visible in the grass. Happy Valley was first named in the early 19th century by the Rector of Ovingdean, Alfred Stead; previous to that it was known as Wick Bottom in 1714.

A similar view taken by Dave Billings in 2000 for the Millennium book on the village.

Downs Road in the late 1920s with no pavements. Passengers for the 14-seat single-deck bus to Rottingdean wait by the roadside before the days of dedicated bus stops. Miss Tullett's gable-fronted bungalow is to the left alongside our family house built in 1948.

Incorrectly titled 'Rottingdean Road', but serves as a reminder as to the confusion over names at the time. The black-boarded bungalow with the pointed roof was called 'Eversglade' and was first occupied by Mr W J Fortescue and later by Mr Ballard who ran a poultry farm. The Ellis family lived there during the 1940s. Mr Ellis was a builder and built several houses in Farm Hill immediately after the war. The Pannett family lived there during the 1950s but had it demolished after they built the present bungalow behind it. After they moved house Kate and May Tullett

took it over. Robin Pannett, a close friend of mine, very sadly passed away in November 2004.

View from Downs Road towards the north-east in the 1920s. The WW1 army huts are visible on the distant skyline.

One of the most iconic photographs of Woodingdean painted by Douglas Holland and much prized by those fortunate to own a print. Thomas Tillings 'Bean' bus service 2B ran from Rottingdean to Elm Grove via the Downs Hotel between 1926 and 1932. There were four identical fourteen-seater vehicles and this one had the registration number PM 7284. See THMP Chapter 4 'Early Bus Services'.

An earlier photograph of Downs Road showing The Nook Poultry Farm and little else behind. Notice the two very ancient tracks running across the hillside and how narrow Downs Road was at the time.

A lovely photograph of Downs Road showing The Nook Poultry Farm during the mid-1920s. The Race Hill development appears partially built on the right. The Warren Farm School's barns are clearly shown centre of picture.

View from the cinder track across Downs Road to the Downs Estate during the 1920s.

Another view of Downs Road probably taken in the early 1930s. The villagers in Rottingdean often referred to this section of the road as the 'Woodingdean Road'.

Disused farm buildings at the top of Falmer Road during the 1930s.

The new Falmer Road shortly after realignment and road widening.

we know today to be the farm and field in the hollow on the Ovingdean Road alongside the Falmer Road. See Map 4 Woodendean Farm page 49 THMP. This small area is now part of Ovingdean village.

Woodendean Farm, although in the parish of Rottingdean, was originally part of Balsdean Farm but sometime in the 17th century 438 acres was separated off to become an independent farm with its own farmhouse bordering on the Ovingdean north-east boundary. In the 1830s a mansion called Woodingdean House was built next door by Thomas Barrett-Lennard Esq MP who lived there until he sold the property to Mr Reuben Terrewest. Lennard chose the name Woodingdean House in order to differentiate its name from Woodendean Farm. It passed through the hands of several owners including William Cowley (1919), Violet Annie Van Der Elst and Thomas Henry Sargent better known as the comedian Max Miller (1939). The Emperor of Ethiopia, Haile Selassie lived there in exile between 1939 and 1941 and the last family to own and live there from 1945 was Roger Jacques Alfonso Vanderborght. It was Vanderborght who changed the name of the house to Woodland Grange possibly because he disliked the name on account of its link with the village being built to the north of him. The property remained until 1965 when it was demolished to make way for a small development of bungalows in Ovingdean Close. The adjacent flint-built farmhouse was latterly converted in the modern fashion.

The following table sets out the owners of Woodendean Farm compiled by John Davies from Land Tax Assessments and Censuses.

1714	Charles Geere
1740	Widow of Charles Geere
1750s	John Paine
1760s	Samuel Ridge
1770	Mrs Ruth Beard
1791	Messrs Whitfield & Co
1793	John Alexander
1794	William Alexander
1800	Messrs Hurley & Co
1809	Stephen Martin
1841	Reuben Terrewest (?)
1852	Charles Beard
1870	Steyning Beard and George Humphrey Beard
1882	Steyning Beard
1913	Brighton Corporation

In 1919 William Cowley purchased the 19-acre part of Woodingdean Farm that was transferred into the Ovingdean parish in 1952.

The Downs Estate occupied an area bounded by Warren Way, Balsdean Road (although not named at the time), Crescent Drive to the east, Occupation Road

Painting of the 1923 landscape by Douglas Holland of his home in Channel View Road when aged about fourteen.

A young Ray Biddle and his father in Rosebury Avenue in the early 1930s. Ray took over the milk round after the War.

Vernon Chandon's dream development captured by Douglas Holland on canvas.

Price's Stores, part of Chandon's grand "Race Hill" scheme. The ESSO Filling Station now occupies the site.

Sam Woolgar's old butcher's shop by this time was being used by Dr Margorie and dentist Peter Southgate and Sam had moved into the three-storey building on the left. Sam had a passion for sea fishing and often joined my grandfather Arthur Tolman on his boat "Redwing" out of Newhaven at a time when quality meat was difficult to buy. Taking his advice Sam left the butchery trade to re-open in Larcombe's Stores as a wet fish shop before his new shop was ready. His son, also Sam, trained as a butcher but followed his father into the fish business. Young Sam was a popular boy in the village and now lives in Somerset.

Race Hill Farm, home of the Chapman family for many years until the 1950s when it was mysteriously demolished by the Brighton Corporation and the foundation stone removed to the Council's yard. See the Chapman family pages 97-102 in THMP. Painting by Douglas Holland.

A pastoral scene by Douglas Holland.

One of the most iconic photographs of Woodingdean painted by Douglas Holland and much prized by those fortunate to own a print. Thomas Tilling's 'Bean' bus service 2B ran from Rottingdean to Elm Grove via the Downs Hotel between 1926 and 1932. There were four identical fourteen-seater vehicles and this one had the registration number PM 7284. See THMP Chapter 4 'Early Bus Services'.

Christmas party in the Village Hall in the late 1920s. It was in this hall that the Downs Sports Club was formed from which grew the Woodingdean Football Club and the Downs Cricket Club in 1926. Tom Newbury, who owned the Happy Corner Café, provided the inspiration for the formation of the cricket club. This is one of the best photographs of the earliest settlers in the village.

A historically priceless painting of the Mission Hall by Douglas Holland with the Pitts bungalow behind on the hill; in the early days there were about forty parishioners.

Lynda Wymark and Dick and Peggy Cuthbertson in 2009 in the garden of where 'The Beehive' once stood. Between them they have lived in the village for over 200 years! Lynda's family have lived in the village since the 1930s when her grandparents Amy and Alfie Elford started a smallholding and a pig farm. Her mother and father Bill and Bunny Ruffle were well known in the village and could often be found in the Happy Corner Café with the Newbury family with whom they were great friends. Bunny was also a great friend of my mother's and on occasions would come along to the Downs Cricket Club matches. When Lynda left school her first thoughts were to work in the village and secure a position at the Post Office in Falmer Road which is where she met her future husband Jack who was working in the garage nearby. They were married in the Church of the Holy Cross in 1970 where later she served as a Churchwarden for seven years. She is still a keen churchgoer, sings in the Church choir and helps out on all occasions particularly when decorating the church with flowers. Jack and Lynda had three children, Alan, Brian and Elaine while living in Brighton for a short time and eight grandchildren. They have lived in Balsdean Road for the last thirty years and their hobbies include gardening and caravanning. Jack helps out on the Vintage London to Brighton Car Run by towing the old crocks up Clayton Hill in his four-wheel vehicle.

Douglas Holland's iconic painting of Warren Farm and the School.

Douglas Holland's interpretation of where the School's barns were situated in relation to the modern Woodingdean Library. They were beautiful barns where children played in the meadow alongside. In the lower picture the School's swimming pool enclosure walls can just be seen between the pair of cottages and the gable-ended barn on the road.

Standean Bottom where cricket was played in the mid-18th Century. In the 1750s cricket was played on 'Basden Flats' between teams from Rottingdean, Lewes and Brighthelmstone. Leading exponents were Thomas Clare, landlord of the White Horse and King of Prussia of Rottingdean, and Thomas Goldsmith, landlord of the Wheatsheaf at Lewes, an old sporting house. In 1758 an account in 'Brighton in the Golden Times' (1880) refers to a cricket match to be held on the 28th June will  be play'd at Rottingdean near Lewes for a guinea a man; Newick, Chailey, Lindfield and Hamsey against Lewes, Brighthelmstone and Rottingdean whose players were John Newington, Stenning Beard, Thomas Clare and Phillip Emery. Not only did landlord Clare play cricket but in May 1758 he advertised to acquaint the public with bull-baiting at his inn in Rottingdean; he also advertised for persons to bring their cocks to fight at five shillings a battle - 'A good Twelvepenny Ordinary at One o'clock'. Rottingdean at the period must have been a lively place! (See cricket THMP pages 252-253)

A group of 'students' of local history sit on the remains of the Manor House wall in 2006. Pat and Len Norris are far left, Lynda Wymark sits fifth from the right in a red top and the author is in the middle in a green shirt.

and Downs Road (later to become the Falmer Road) and was sited on the former Woodendean Farm. Valley Road (later Downs Valley Road) and The Ridgway were incorporated within its boundaries. No part of the Estate lay on either, Balsdean, Norton or Wick Farms. The development was advertised nationally and called the "Brighton Downs Estate" although locally it was simply the Downs Estate. The developers were Percy Harvey Estates Ltd., of 46, Queen Victoria Street, London who acted through their subsidiary the Brighton Downs Estate Ltd. Solicitors to both were Mackrell & Co of Cannon St, London.

Title of the Downs Estate commenced with a conveyance eight days before the company was registered at Companies House in April 1913. Title to part of the land which lay in the parish of Rottingdean commenced with an Indenture of Mortgage dated the 14th October 1885 made between Steyning Beard and the Rev. Carey Hampton Borrer and the Rev. Charles Alexander Borrer. For the other part laying in the parish of Ovingdean it commenced with an Indenture of Conveyance dated 30th October 1891 made between Chester Macnaghten and others and Frederick Charsley. Purchasers of the plots were entitled to an abstract of the title on payment of one guinea but were not able to make any objections to it.

Percy Harvey Estates also offered similar developments at East Grinstead, Chatham, Caterham, Burgess Hill, Dorking, Horley and in north Devon. All the estates were for residential purposes but only the Downs Estate offered ample ground for orchards and paddocks all at 'absolute value and low prices'. They also offered small "land-locked" parcels of land, both arable and pasture for smallholders and could advise as to the suitability for poultry, fruit culture, vegetable produce and marketing. The estate was described as being 'adjacent to land recently (1913) acquired by the Corporation of Brighton for public purposes and within two and a half miles of a railway station', - most probably Falmer. The soil was described as being rich loam over well-drained chalk. It would have been these last qualities that probably drew people's attention to the Downs Estate as many of the early purchasers and settlers became poultry farmers and smallholders growing both fruit and vegetables for sale either on site or at the Brighton markets. These smaller parcels of land to which they referred were available in several locations, namely three, 3-acre plots on the east side of The Ridgway, one 2-acre plot and nineteen 1-acre plots fronting Valley Road. This layout explains why so many smallholders and poultry farmers favoured that side of the village. The developers also offered one 3-acre site at the bottom of Downs Road on the bend, and twenty-four 1-acre plots sandwiched also between The Ridgway and Downs Road. This also explains why the layout of Falmer Gardens and several other 'mini estates' within that particular area eventually developed in the way they did. It also explains the layout of the later development of the land between The Ridgway and Valley Road and possibly the difficulties experienced later on in selling the land after owners had further divided or split up the partially developed plots. It is known

THE
BRIGHTON DOWNS ESTATE.

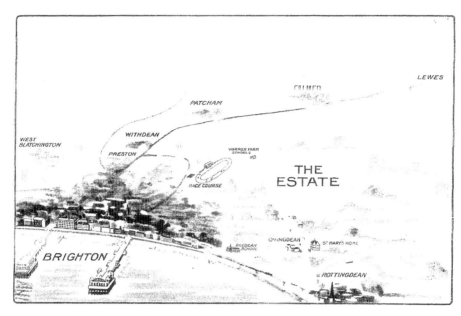

PANORAMIC VIEW SHEWING ESTATE.

PLEASE ADDRESS ALL ENQUIRIES :—

PERCY HARVEY ESTATES, Ltd.,
46, QUEEN VICTORIA STREET, LONDON, E.C. 4.

Telephone : Bank 41.

SOLICITORS : MESSRS. MACKRELL & CO., 21, CANNON STREET, LONDON, E.C. 4.

The 'Brighton Downs Estate' Conditions of Sale and Contract used by Percy Harvey Estates Ltd for the promotion of their land sales in 1919 many years before the area became known as 'Woodingdean'.

that ownership of a few plots in the vicinity were claimed by possessionary title and that owners' names were disputed.

The Downs Estate consisted of 528 individual building plots each with 'road' frontage and, except for twelve plots earmarked for shops at the top of Downs Road, most were 40x200 feet or nearly a fifth of an acre in size. There were a number of larger one-acre plots offered all along Crescent Drive. The standard forty-foot-wide plots on Downs Road in 1920 were offered for £40 each and those on the other roads for £30. In 1948 my parents purchased a plot on the Falmer Road for a few hundred pounds and in 1958 the adjacent vacant plot was sold by Kate and May Tullett for around £800, the same plot by 2008 had risen to £100,000 or more. By 1926 the price of a plot in The Ridgway had risen to £35 or to the equivalent of about twelve weeks' wages.

By 1920 all the larger parcels of land on the estate had been sold along with 52 standard plots on Downs Road and 45 on The Ridgway. On the Valley Road all had been sold except for seven larger one-acre plots along the east side. The 1920 original site layout of the estate shows Valley Road with a bend on the north end where joining Crescent Drive and The Ridgway as having a pronounced curve at the southern end. When finally laid, however, the layout of those roads had been changed as they appear today.

Only one or two dwellings were to be allowed on each plot and each purchaser was required to conform to strict stipulations and conditions as to the building and the land. Purchasers were required to erect a fence three feet six inches high not closer than 20 feet from the centre of the road, the developers having previously staked out the boundary. The building line for all the dwellings was established as a minimum of 40 feet also from the centre of the road. Only private houses were to be built and no huts, caravans or houses on wheels were permitted. Houses were to be built to a minimum cost standard, £225 if upon the Downs Road, The Ridgway or Crescent Drive, or £400 for a pair of semi-detached houses, or £175 for a detached and £340 for a pair of semi-detached if on the Valley Road. Plans of the dwelling had to be approved by the developer or their surveyor for which a fee of 10s 6d for each set of plans was charged. By 1926 the cost standard had risen to £600 for the Downs Road, The Ridgway and Crescent Drive or £575 if semi-detached and £450 on the Valley Road and £400 for the semis. For the purpose of substantiating cost it was stated 'the cost of every house and other buildings shall be taken to be the net first cost thereof in labour and material alone estimated at the lowest current prices'. They further said that no terraced houses would be permitted without the previous written consent of the vendors. It was not until the mid-1960s that the first Local Authority terraced houses appeared on the estate. Other than horticulture, poultry farming or fruit growing no trade could be carried out at the property. Any portion of the plot which lay within twenty feet of the centre of the road was reserved for the roadway and footpaths and every purchaser would have to pay a road charge according to the frontage and cost. The developers, however, reserved the right to alter or waive all or any of these stipulations and conditions when laying out the estate.

Purchasers were required to put down a 10% deposit on the cost of their plot and then had three months to pay the balance failing which interest was chargeable at 6% per annum; however, if the purchaser fell ill and was able to show positive proof then an extension of time would be permitted. Any unpaid balance of the purchase money could be recovered by the vendors with interest. One of the first purchasers of land on the Downs Estate was Harold Price who was living in Chiswick, London having recently returned from India where he had been on active service with the 10th Middlesex Regiment. Harold's parents had already moved to the Downs Estate in 1918 and Harold was shortly to follow. In December 1919 Harold bought six plots, nos 115 to 120 on The Ridgway for £165 0s 0d, most probably the largest single purchase at the time. See pages 113-117 of THMP for the story of the Price family.

In 1917 there were only seventeen families living in the whole of Woodingdean and by 1923 only fifty-eight, half of whom lived on this estate, including the five families living on Downs Road. In the same year sixteen families were designated ploughmen, poultry farmers and farmers. There were two shopkeepers on the Downs Road, Miss Elizabeth Sleightholm and Mr Albert R Stowell. Miss Sleightholm had the first small general stores on the corner opposite the Downs Hotel and Albert Stowell had his Emporium a little further down where the garage is today. (see page 49 of WR&TM). Both Harold Price and Albert Stowell acted in turn as local land agents for the Brighton Downs Estate Ltd picking up potential buyers from Brighton station and showing them around the estate, preferably when the weather was at its best. Harold was a poultry farmer and looking to start a garage, and Albert the Emporium from which he sold second-hand furniture, very popular with many of the early settlers. As they were already running their own small businesses in the village they were both set to prosper. Photographs of the original parade of shops at the top of Downs Road show the two large signs on the crossroads advertising this and the Brighton Heights Estate land for sale.

By 1925 twenty-six families lived on the Downs Estate but by 1930 this had increased to ninety-one in The Ridgway, Valley Road, Balsdean Road and Crescent Drive. A further twenty-nine lived above and below the Downs Hotel. All told there were 230 dwellings and 30 commercial enterprises in the village. Up until 1926 any family living north of Warren Road was listed as living on that road. In 1938 there were about 520 dwellings in Woodingdean. In 1978 the area of the whole village was some 430 acres of which eighty-three percent was on the former Woodendean Farm and seventeen percent on the former Norton and Wick Farms.

Road adoption was slow to say the least as was the provision of main services.

In the early days water was either collected from a standpoint on the green opposite the Downs Hotel or was delivered to the door by Arnold Pitteway who lived at the top of The Ridgway. The majority of families constructed their own water collection system whereby they were able to filter rainwater directly from the roof through sand, for storage in a tank alongside or in the house. Dick Cuthbertson, who lives in Balsdean Road, remembers this only to well. The early residents had to wait many years until piped water was made available. Similarly it was not until the 1930s that main drainage was connected on the first part of the estate. People living on the south side of Crescent Drive had to wait longer. Only The Ridgway, Downs Road and the north end of Crescent Drive was made up and adopted with paved footpaths before WWII. People living on the south end of Crescent Drive, Valley Road and Balsdean Road had to wait until the 1950s before they could drive cars on a road to their house or set foot on a proper footpath. Before that their roads were narrow muddy tracks often impassable during the winter months.

A more comprehensive history of the development of the Downs Estate and also of the issues raised at Public hearings is told in Chapter 1 of THMP.

◂o▸◂o▸◂o▸

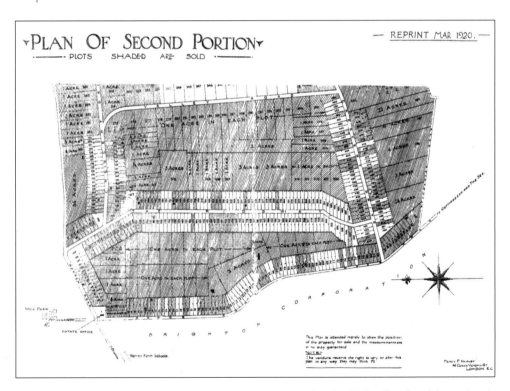

Plan of the second portion of the Downs Estate from Downs Road to Valley Road and the curiously named Occupation Road in 1920. Note the size of some of the back plots.

Downs Road and Downs Valley Road

The cutting of Kipling Avenue in 1946 in preparation for the building of prefabricated bungalows as a way of alleviating the housing shortage after the war. They were intended as a short term remedy but they were not taken down until the 1960s. Notice the large expanse of land between The Ridgway and Downs Valley Road on which can be seen Mr Fairley's poultry houses.

Construction of the prefabs is underway in this photograph taken in 1946. The prefabricated sections were made in Bristol and came in by low-loaders one of which was involved in a bad accident with a car on the crossroads. Notice the haystack on Downs Valley Road and the wide open spaces behind.

A very tidy housing estate in about 1950.

Very tidy homes not many years after the War.

70

Downs Valley Road in the 1930s. Already ruins of older buildings were beginning to appear.

Disused pigsties on the Downs Estate, a leftover from the very early days of homestead farming.

A collapsing bungalow overtaken by mother nature.

Early DIY, alterations or demolition!

An early timber garage on Downs Valley Road in the 1930s. There would not have been a road in front of the property at the time.

The ranging rods may be being used to set out a new house with Downs Valley Road in the background. Notice the haystacks, a very common sight in the earlier days of the village.

Geese were a very common sight and acted as watch dogs. This photograph was taken by Ray Biddle who grew up in the village.

VALLEY ESTATE,
WOODINGDEAN
AYING WATER MAINS FOR SUN TRAP VILLAS
THE GANGSTERS IN POSSESSION.

Laying the water main on the Valley Estate in the late 1930s with a young John Martin standing in front of his father. The workmen were all from the Brighton Waterworks Co.

The Ridgway

Top of The Ridgway looking north-east showing a house on the skyline alongside an old flint pit and two Nissen huts used by the Canadian Army during WWI. The huts were later stripped of timber cladding and used to build 'The Beehive' the home of the Cuthbertson family in the mid-1920s. Harold Price's first Garage can be seen on The Ridgway and three houses on Balsdean Road. The field at the top is part of the Brighton Heights Estate.

The Ridgway and the Downs Estate in the mid-1920s showing only a few bungalows and lots of open space.

The Ridgway in about 1923.

Dennis Fairley's poultry farm.

The same year. The first bungalow and the barn on the right was a dairy run by the Hardiment brothers who lived further up the road. In the dip of the road there was a duck pond which was eventually filled in to facilitate traffic. The Chapman's family bungalow is second up on the left. Walter Chapman lived in Race Hill Farm at the top of Wilson Avenue from 1914 when aged three. William and Sarah West and their daughter Doris bought the bungalow shown in the picture from Mr Littlejohn, the builder, for £550 in 1926. See the story of The Chapmans THMP pages 97 -102.

Dennis Fairley's poultry farm between The Ridgway and Downs Valley Road before the war. The track to the right could be used when the "road" was impassable; a case of do as you like.

Crescent Drive

One of the oldest photographs of the village taken on the first day of snow in 1920 showing Mr Martin (probably the milkman) outside the Bakery (unknown) in Crescent Drive.

Crescent Drive in the early 1920s. Notice the haystack near Balsdean Road and 'The Beehive', the home of the Cuthbertson family.

One or two more houses in this photograph but urbanisation was slow during the depression of the 1920s. A lonely walker strides out for home.

The Downs Estate in 1927 with the footprint of Valley Road (the 'Downs' was added later) beginning to take shape. The long white building right of centre at the top of The Ridgway was the Village Hall, sometimes called the Sports Hall. It is known that the land on the Downs Estate was not cultivated for a number of years before being sold as building land.

Crescent Drive in 1928 when poultry farming was made popular by suggestions offered by the Downs Estate Company which introduced the concept in their conditions of sale. By 1930 there were only fifty-five families living around Crescent Drive.

The road is dry and summer bonfires abound.

Christmas party in the Village Hall in the late 1920s. It was in this hall that the Downs Sports Club was formed from which grew the Woodingdean Football Club and the Downs Cricket Club in 1926. Tom Newbury, who owned the Happy Corner Café, provided the inspiration for the formation of the cricket club. This is one of the best photographs of the earliest settlers in the village.

Crescent Drive North in 1937. Road adoption ceased on the outbreak of War, on the far bend in the road, but was continued later in the 1950s.

Crescent Drive South in the early 1950s when new bungalows began to appear on the north side of the road.

Crescent Drive South in the early 1950s showing some of the original bungalows built in the 1920s.

Crescent Drive South in the early 1950s before the road was adopted. Possibly taken in 1952, the year in which identity cards were abandoned - introduced during WWII as a way of protecting the nation from Nazi spies.

A similar view about the same time.

Another similar view at the same time.

Crescent Drive North before the road was adopted.

Crescent Drive North at the junction with Heronsdale Road near to where the road had been made up before the war. Note the street lamp.

The Kitson family bungalow on Crescent Drive overlooked by modern houses on Balsdean Road. This bungalow was one of the original homes built on the Downs Estate. Mr Kitson had a greengrocers shop on Warren Road for many years having arrived in the village during the 1920s.

Mr Smith's bungalow at the junction of Crescent Drive North and Downs Valley Road after German bombing on Sunday 9th March 1941. Mr Smith's donkey was killed in the raid.

"Ung" and "En"

Why was the village called Woodingdean when for centuries the area had been called either Norton, Wick or Warren as in farms or the Downs Estate or even the Brighton Downs and then why was the 'ing' adopted and not the original and faithful spelling with the 'en' as in Woodendean Farm which founded it? According to John Davies, Woodingdean Farm existed from before 1714 to about 1979, its farmhouse being called Woodingcote. Both the farmhouse and farmlands lay in the Rottingdean parish, then in 1952 the farm buildings were transferred into the Ovingdean parish. The original name of the farm was Woodendean (i.e. wooded valley) Farm, a name which arose from the woods which once covered the east side of Long Hill, Beacon Hill and Creek Bottom. These woods linger on today, and are very evident in old photographs of the area.

The earliest record seen by John Davies and Professor Richard Coates of this farm is on Glover's plan dating from 1714 which includes a symbolic drawing of a small thatched farmhouse in the Balsdean part of Rottingdean parish with the note "The lands of Charles GEERE called Base Den Farme". The original Woodingdean House and cottages date from before 1839. The earliest record of the name Woodendean appears in the Rottingdean vestry minutes dated 1784 (ESRO PAR 466 9/2) but the 1783 map only marks an un-named farmhouse. The 1789 2" OS map shows 'Wooderdean'(sic) in a preliminary survey but the 1813 1" OS map reverts to "-endean". William Figg's 1819 map of Challoners records Wooden-dean Farm and Greenwoods map of 1825 shows Woodendon Farm. Robson's Commercial Directory of 1839 spells it Woodenden.

The 1839 Tithe map records the name Wooden Dean (ESRO TD/E 152) and two years later in 1841 the census records the name Woodendean. However, whilst the Rottingdean electoral lists of 1841-73 (ESRO QDE/3/E.1-45) records the name Woodingdean the same parish registers of 1848-1912 records the more consistent Woodendean.(ESRO PAR 466/1/2/2, /3/2) Woodingdean again appears in John Dudeney's diary of 1849 (ESRO ACC 3785/3 and 4) and the very unusual name of Wootingde(a)n is used in Melville's directory of 1858. In 1862 Woodendean re-appears in Wyld's plan, Volunteer Review dated 21st April 1862 (BAL local map 24). In that same year the Sussex historian John Erredge spells it with "ing." The 1874-95 Ovingdean baptismal register and the

1878-81 Rottingdean electoral lists uses "en" but the Ovingdean parish baptismal register in 1889-95 reverted to using "ing" but only after overwriting the "en" as though it were a second thought or a correction. In 1890 Kelly's directory also uses "ing". In 1931 Woodendene,-dean is used by Thirkell.

After 1939, Pike's Street directory persists with Woodende(a)n whilst Kelly's continues with the "ing". According to Professor Coates, in a frequent local pronunciation, the final syllable is stressed as with *Rottingdean* and *Ovingdean.*

Professor Coates suggests in an earlier article of his, and to which I referred in THMP (pages 48-51), that the name appears to be an eighteenth-century invention on a model of Rottingdean and Ovingdean. Spellings in 'en' were frequent for Rottingdean at this period and reflect the authentic local pronunciation with *-ing /-en* appearing to be a spelling-based upgrade like that seen in the modern pronunciation of Rottingdean itself. If there was some verbal humour relating *Wood-en-dean* to *Rottendean,* it is hard to pin down precisely how. It has been suggested that the spelling 'ing' may be a deliberate alteration by Sir Thomas Barrett-Lennard on his taking over the house in 1888, a view shared by John Davies; but it is found in published form already in Erredge (1862), unpublished earlier still in Dudeney's diary and in electoral registers (uniquely, as a class of documents), and in an otherwise badly mistaken form in

Woodingdean House built around 1830 once occupied by William Cowley between 1919-29 who gave his name to 'Cowley Drive'. The house was known as Woodendean House up to about 1888, then Woodingdean House until 1937, and when comedian Max Miller, the 'Cheeky Chappie', took it over in 1939 he cheekily changed its name to Woodland Grange, but a grange it never was. It was demolished in 1965. Woodingdean Farm on the left existed before 1714 and was originally known as Woodendean farm.

Melville's (1858). Professor Coates says that John Davies may well be right in speculating that Barrett-Lennard was decisive in making the name-change effective; perhaps the baronet thought *Wooden*-sounded undignified and perhaps he had already read Erredge.

The change to the name of the house was probably made by T H Sargent, alias Max Miller the comedian, who lived there and may have felt that the name had been tainted by its association with the plot land development.

Professor Coates states that because of what look likes snobbery in renaming the house, also lies the very occasional use of the name North Rottingdean instead of Woodingdean. Whilst I have not heard this particular name it is true that a number of people living on the Falmer Road said that they lived in Rottingdean; this, however, may have been for other reasons, namely that Falmer Road was previously Downs Road and before that it was known as Rottingdean Road and some of those residents were in place at that time. According to Professor Coates the name Woodingdean appears in the nearest arable field of East Side Farm to the site of Woodingdean Laine, the triangular field east of the Falmer Road and opposite The Vale. This he says was the site of The Nine Acres and Wardean Brow on Glover's plan of Ovingdean Manor Farm. North of this field is the remnant of what the late resident Jim Roberts once referred to as the Woodingdean Copse frequented by gypsies before Falmer Road was developed.

The name Woodingdean had been established for the original farm site but still no name had yet been established for the plot land development springing up as two new estates in the north known as Wick and Downs Estates, perceived *"as a potato patch in the wilds"* by the Sussex Daily News in 1929. Indeed there was actually a third estate called the Brighton Heights Estate but that one met with only partial success. It must be said that the standard of building and the generous plot sizes on the Wick and Downs Estates were far superior to those of Lancing and Peacehaven where a standard plot was only twenty-two and a half-feet wide. Although the July 1915 Conditions of Sale published by the Brighton Downs Estate for the sale of the land frequently referred to the land as being in the parish of Rottingdean or near to Ovingdean nowhere does it refer to the name Woodingdean. Even the sales particulars refer to the estate as being adjacent to the Estate recently acquired by the Brighton Corporation, that is, Happy Valley. It is clear that the name Woodingdean was not in use at the time by the developers. The slogan *"panoramic view shewing the estate"* used by Percy Harvey Estates on the front cover of their sales particulars shows Rottingdean and Ovingdean quite clearly but the space where Woodingdean is located is described as "The Estate". See illustration page 66. One might think that their Solicitors Messrs Mackrell & Co would have been pedantic enough to clarify the location name if it were available at the time. Clearly there must have been some confusion in the minds of the residents living on the Downs or the Wick Estates as to the name of the areas in which they were living. It must be remembered, of course, that all the early settlers arrived within a few years of each other, Harold Price being one of the earliest in 1919 when he purchased six plots on The Ridgway. In 1920 Harold's family purchased Nicholl's bunglow opposite their house and renamed the bungalow "Rovingdean". Perhaps this was the forerunner to naming the village, because by this time Harold Price had already been appointed the local agent for the Downs Estate Company whose remoteness in London may have left them unconcerned as to what name was given to the village. By 1923 Harold was making steady progress with several businesses and being an entrepreneur and organiser was co-opted with Eustace Gibson, a chemist, who had a small shop near the crossroads, to join the Rottingdean parish council in 1925 in order to represent the people on the Downs and Wick estates. At the same time the then owner of Woodingdean House, Alderman William A Cowley, may have been asked for his consent for the developers to use the name Woodingdean for the Downs Estate since Cowley had once owned the land. Did then Harold Price and Eustace Gibson suggest the adoption of the name Woodingdean to the Downs Estate Company, remembering that Harold was their agent, or did Harold and Eustace simply suggest the name to Chairman Lang of the Rottingdean parish council who may then have made the suggestion to Alderman Cowley? We shall see later but clearly the residents wanted a name for their plot land development and this may have been the best way of getting it for the entire area of the Wick, Downs and the Brighton Heights Estates. The developer's 1919 plan of the Wick Estate shows the land as being at Race Hill, Brighton, not Woodingdean.

It could now be said that very few villages in recent times have been named by the villagers themselves. Both the place names Rottingdean and Ovingdean go back to Domesday albeit name changes have taken place over the centuries.

Harold and Eustace join the Council and the village gets its name

On the 8th July 1925, at a meeting of the Rottingdean Parish Council, the Clerk, J. George Wright, reported on a letter that he had received from the East Sussex County Council dated 20th May 1925 asking for further particulars in regard to the creation of a new Ward in the parish. George Wright replied *"That part of the Parish of Rottingdean north of the point on High Hill where the boundaries of Ovingdean Parish and Iford Parish adjoin"* and gave the Committee the number of electors in the Parish as follows:-

Black Rock Ward	170
Rottingdean	640
Proposed new Ward	380

The East Sussex County Council said that the name of the new Ward would be called *"The Downs Ward".* and that *"Two additional Parish Councillors to be allotted and a map defining the new Ward to be forwarded".*

On the occasion of the next Parish meeting on the 7th October 1925 it was resolved -

"... the Order of the East Sussex County Council dated 28th July 1925 dividing Parish into three Wards and increasing the number of Parish Councillors from 11 to 13 was read and the Clerk was instructed to make the necessary arrangements for the election of two Parish Councillors from the Downs Ward".

At the 205th meeting of the Rottingdean Parish Council in the schoolroom at Rottingdean on the 14th December 1925 there were ten parish councillors present under the chairmanship of RCV Lang MA (who lived at St Aubyns School) to hear the Clerk report that, as a result of the Parish meeting in the Downs Ward for the election of two Parish Councillors a poll had been demanded and an election had duly been held on the 20th November 1925 at which there were four candidates. The votes cast were:-

Cummings, Alan Tweedie	20
Gibson, Eustace Gordon	148
Hardiment, Alfred Arthur	66
Price, Harold Edwin	111

The Returning Officer duly declared Messrs Gibson and Price as elected and the Chairman extended to them a hearty welcome to which each of the new members made suitable replies. The declarations accepting offices were duly signed and witnessed for Woodingdean Ward.

This point in time is very important for it marked a small piece of history, the recording for the first time that two Councillors were elected to represent both the Wick and Downs Estates on the Rottingdean Parish Council and for the first time the words *"Downs Ward"* and subsequently *"Woodingdean Ward"* had probably been recorded at a Parish Council meeting.

To establish the validity of this historical point meant trawling through many years of Parish Council Minutes to see whether or not there had been any previous mention or recording of either name, the Downs Estate or Woodingdean or whether there had been any discussion between the Councillors on the affairs of the northerly and largely forgotten areas of their own parish. We shall see what Eustace and Harold did at their first and subsequent meetings later, before that we turn back the clock ten years to 1915.

This particular Rottingdean Parish Council minute book opens on the 23rd September 1915 with Councillor S M Moens in the chair. It is worth mentioning here that Col Moens lived at Dene Cottage and author of the book "Rottingdean" in 1952. There are another seven Councillors present and all are discussing the very untidy state of the village so much so that they accepted a tender from A&EW Moppett for £115 for scavenging work plus 10d per load of water to wash the streets. Even Miss Lawrence, owner of Roedean School, promised to help clean up the street litter. There were serious discussions early in 1916 about the continuing cost of the sea defence works and because of the shortage of manpower Messrs Margetts and Cooke, the village builders, could not complete their work, also that there was the possibility of Geisha Cottage falling into the sea.

Enlisted men were listed for posterity in the summer of 1916 and few meetings were to take place. Col Moens departed to Mesopotamia on war service in 1916 and in 1917 it was again recorded that repairing sea walls and groynes was a continuous task at great cost to the ratepayers. It is worth remembering that this was before the construction of the undercliff walk during the 1930s. The Committee were also preoccupied with road repairs around the village pond. Such were the high costs of the work the Council resorted to a loan from the East Sussex County Council towards the expense of maintaining the sea defences at Rottingdean and along the Brighton Road. The severity of this situation in and around the village occupied a great deal of their voluntary time leaving little time to think about the forgotten area to the north which by this time was beginning to have its own problems. In 1918 a new problem arose for the Committee to sort out. Thomas Tilling, the bus company, had advised the Council that due to the petrol shortage a reduction in services was imminent and would present serious consequences for the village. Whilst they discussed points of this nature there remained no discussion on the problems besetting the local farmers who employed many of the villagers.

The high cost of repairing the sea defences rumbled on putting a financial stranglehold on the community to the extent that the Council reluctantly asked the County Council to step in and finance a £4,000 repair contract. On the 25th March 1919 it was resolved to issue a Precept on the Overseers for the sum of £170 to meet general expenses of the Council for the next six months under the Local Government Act 1894.

The spiralling costs of providing public services in the village were of great concern necessitating the Council to instruct the Rottingdean Electric Company to turn off the public lamps without endangering the public. Sea defence expenditure was such that the Council applied to the Newhaven Rural District Council for a loan of £2,000 in June 1919. The Peace Day celebrations brought a slight relief in the summer when the Council became preoccupied with welcoming back Col Moens from war service, whereupon he became chairman again in August of that year. Raising an increase of 2d in the rates for serious repairs to the Newhaven Road was one of the first things he tackled on his return. Later, in 1919, the Council again voted to raise £170 for general expenditure at a time when the rising cost of coal and electricity for the nineteen street lamps would be £80 a year. Hard negotiations followed, a reduction of £5 was agreed but the villagers had no lights during the summer. A rather unusual meeting was held on the 26th February 1920 as Miss Lawrence was invited to attend in order to gauge opinion on the proposal for the construction of a high-speed railway in the Ovingdean Valley intended only as an experiment and that the matter of a connection to Brighton, questionable. Miss Lawrence could readily see the benefit for her school to be linked to a railway but the Council agreed that it would not be in the best interest of Rottingdean Parish and rejected it.

Throughout 1920 the councillors were fighting the intrusion of the sea at both ends, and in the centre of the parish, and Mr Horton Ledger notified the Council of his intention to sell the allotment land at Park Place, a sanctuary for working people to grow their own produce. This was deeply unpopular with the allotment holders and the problem rolled on for several months along with the problems of the troublesome gas lights at Black Rock (extreme end of the parish) which kept blowing out due to improper repairs and causing a public nuisance. Raising money to pay for the continuing cost of running the parish was high on the agenda and in March 1920 it was decided to introduce regulations and licensing for hiring out deck chairs, bathing tents and boats, the agreed rate for a chair being 2d for a four-hour period or 3d if it had a canopy. Charges for bathing tents were 6d for an adult and 2d for a child. People with their own tents were to be charged a shilling a day. Tenders for these services were very disappointing with only one submitted by Mr Titchenor for £12 12s 0d, so a re-tender was ordered unless Mr Titchenor increased his tender to £50. After some deliberation Mr Titchenor reluctantly agreed to pay the Council £20 to provide the service on condition that he also acted as Beach Inspector free of charge on behalf of the Committee. Meanwhile, the saga over the loss of the allotments continued throughout the summer but the holders were reprimanded for dumping rubbish on the roadway. Three acres of land were found at Court Ord for the new allotments but were rejected; however, the Rural District Council said that they also could make three acres available in the area. Mr Ledger was most probably feeling the effect of all this pressure as he came up with an offer to re-lease the land for £1500 to the Council. The Allotment Association retired to consider the matter and two of their holders Mr Dudeney and Mr Stenning were ticked off for allowing their allotments to become overgrown with weeds. The Association offered one shilling and sixpence for a rod frontage and Horton Ledger predictably turned it down. To settle the matter the Marquis of Abergavenny agreed to make land above Hog Plat on Windmill Hill available on a fourteen year agreement. At the same time Horton Ledger was holding other negotiations which resulted in him finally agreeing to have eight houses built his on Park Place site in order that the ratepayers be saved the special rate in meeting the cost of a new sewer. At any rate it was agreed by all that the site was an eyesore and something needed to be done. Meanwhile, the Parish Council were concerning themselves with the repairs to the cliff top fencing on the Roedean Road.

Nowhere in the Minutes during the years between 1915 and 1921 is there any mention whatsoever of the Downs Estate or the name Woodingdean but it is easy to see why, the Council was very hard up, they were all working hard and unpaid except the Clerk, Mr Wright, who had a small salary, and the people of Rottingdean were simply not interested in helping or paying for anything to the north of their village. Very understandable and the situation would not be resolved until 1928.

In 1914 Warren Farm School was the only establishment listed by Pikes Brighton Directory (published annually in April of each year) as being in Rottingdean. In 1917 three people are listed, Philip Bailey, Alfred Hardiment in Ridgeway House and Mrs Mason in Ridge Hall all on the Downs Estate and Mr Beard in Wick Farm and Richard Beck in Wick Farm cottage. By 1921 only Mr Hardiment and Mrs Mason are listed as well as Mr Beard. Mr Beecher is listed at Norton Cottage and Scantlebury and Percy in Balsdean and Norton Farms. Three years later in 1924 there are 23 residences on the Downs Estate, 10 on the Warren Road, 4 on Downs Road, 1 on Race Hill Estate, 2 shops Mrs Sleightholme and Mr Stowell, 5 poultry farmers and 1 dairy farmer. Downs Estate is clearly mentioned but Wick Estate and the word Woodingdean are not. In 1926 the name Woodingdean is mentioned but only in the context of a house name, i.e Woodingdean House at the top of Warren Hill. A few families are listed on the Downs Estate and for the first time Falmer Road and Crescent Drive are also mentioned. All houses lying north of Warren Road are listed as being on Warren Road. Henry Peel whose farm gave its name to Farm Hill was a case in point. Wick Farm is not mentioned but Wick Farm Cottage opposite the bottom of Channel View Road is. Interestingly, George Henry Pearson is listed as living at 5 Race Hill, the original parade of shops between McWilliam and Vernon Avenue where the Esso station now stands. The 1927 directory fails to mention a number of families and shopkeepers who are known to have been living there and there is still no mention of the adopted village name Woodingdean. However, Channel View Road is included for the first time and with other roads previously mentioned it shows that these were adopted before the village was finally named.

The 1928 directory mentions Woodingdean and Downs Road for the first time, included quite rightfully as being part of the Downs Estate and although Mrs Chapman's Confectionery shop, Mr Goodenough, the Postmaster and general storekeeper and Slater's Stores had been there for quite sometime this was the first year they were included. By this time Edward and Tilley Larcombe's Grocery Stores, Mrs Parker's General Stores and the butchers Thrower and Woolgar are now listed on Warren Road and the name Race Hill had been dropped. The listings were very unreliable that year. Kelly's Brighton Directory differed somewhat to Pikes but followed similar lines with some unreliable listings and the occasional mention of the word Woodingdean but again only in the context of either a house or road name.

Early in 1921 the dispute over the new allotments in Rottingdean was resolved when nineteen applicants were allocated twenty-nine plots for a shilling a rod but the East Sussex County Council became concerned about the lack of social life in the parish and asked the Councillors for suggestions on formulating a scheme for the development of "Rural Industries and Social Life" in the village. The Councillors were most probably upset by this as they would see it as a reflection on their inability to run a happy village; however, after some discussion they replied that they were thinking of building a village hall anyway, as they said they were a seaside holiday resort and a quiet one at that.

William Cowley, owner of Woodendean Farm, joined the Council to replace Mr Howell in February of the same year and being a farmer one might have expected to see some references being made in the Minutes to the rather forgotten rural farming area north of Rottingdean, but alas this was not to be, even after he was quickly elected Chairman only three months later was there any reference to his farm.

During the following year the Council battled on facing the irritated Mr Titchenor who complained that his takings were well down due to someone in the village hiring out bathing tents and that he was being sabotaged by spilt tar on the steps down to the beach. Mr Pannett the haulier and Mr Albert West the farmer were invited to submit tenders to clear out the village pond, Pannett's tender of £40 based on 200 loads won him the job but afterwards he said he had removed 405 loads and "demanded consideration". The Council's offer of £50 was turned down so they sent him a cheque for £60 saying the amount was beyond their budget. Painting the village seats became a problem but the Clerk said he knew an old man who would work for a shilling an hour if brushes were supplied. A big vote followed and seven Councillors said yes, unfortunately they also voted for a reduction of £150 in the Clerk's salary. The Assistant Overseer also lost a similar amount from his salary. One great decision they arrived at in November was to ask the schoolmaster Mr Sykes to tell the children not to throw stones into the pond!

Budgets were being exceeded and concern was rising over the high costs of bus fares that resulted in the Council demanding that Tillings lower the 8d fare to Brighton on the grounds of cheaper petrol and a fall in the drivers' wages. Tillings dismissed the whole idea but after three months of wrangling they backed down and reduced the fare. Smelly toilets in the White Horse, smelly pigs on Park Place and blocked gullies in the High Street occupied their minds in early 1922 and such was the shortage of funds they sent Mr Filkins the farmer a bill for £3 15s 0d for putting out a haystack fire on his farm. Mr Titchenor got the contract for the hire of the bathing huts and after Mr Lang took over the chairmanship they wrote with tongue in cheek to the Board of Admiralty requesting that they repair the old mill as it was charted for admiralty purposes. The Board replied that they could not help and that if the Council would like to repair the mill themselves they would not mind, besides which "in future navigational charts the mill will be shown in ruins". By September Mr Cowley had dealt with the pigs but the saga of the old mill had drifted on until Mr Gainsford of the Estates Office at Eridge wrote to the Council suggesting that the mill be demolished as it posed a danger to people sitting beneath it. Whilst the proposal was being considered, Mr Gainsford secretly wrote to Margetts and Cooke instructing them to demolish it; however, this leaked out and public representations forced the decision into abeyance, with the Council announcing that no public money could be spent on repairing the mill and any such work could only be done by voluntary subscription. The Abergavenny Estate eventually relented as later in the year they told the Council that they could lease the mill and the land for £5 0s 0d a year for 99 years with the proviso that if the mill ceased to exist then the land must revert to the Estate.

By now the parish land which was to create the Wick and Downs Estates had been sold but no mention of either transaction had been discussed by the Council or brought to their attention or at least if it had then they were not discussing it in public. The sale of nearly nine hundred acres of "Rottingdean land" or about a third of the parish simply went unrecorded as though the matter didn't exist. The ramifications of what was happening in the north of the parish with the uncontrolled sale of plot lands and the erection of only medium quality housing stock on some of the roads would have a significant and profound effect on the history of the parish. There seems to have been no control over the development by the Newhaven Rural District Council as to what could or should be built on either of the two estates. All the planning approvals given by the District Council in the early 1920s were given quickly and without any consideration as to architectural merit or build quality, only perhaps to the cost limitation previously mentioned. There seems to be no record as to whether those cost limitations were imposed on the new owners at the outset by the District Council or by the Percy Harvey Estates as a way of maintaining or enhancing their own standards. Whether similar cost limitations were imposed on their other estates such as at East Grinstead is unknown. Meanwhile, whilst all this was going on, the Rottingdean Parish Council occupied their time with more trivial matters such as whether Mr King the fireman at Black Rock should or should not be fitted out with a uniform.

By now it was 1923 and still there was no representation on the Council by people from either of the two estates and certainly no formal name had been given to that part of their parish. The Council were more interested in supporting a motion put forward by the Borough of Lowestoft to petition the Government to accept coastal defence work as a national charge. Money was in short supply and they were in debt to the East Sussex County Council, expenditure was over budget by 16% and they were forced to rely on income from the bathing machines and the allotments to balance the budget. Income from the latter was set to rise by nearly four pounds the following year because someone had undermeasured the land area. The additional income was crucial. On the downside Messrs Tamplins the brewers were dumping all sorts of material on their land as to make it an eyesore. Matters got a little out of control in the autumn when the Council ordered the removal of advertising boards along the Brighton Road and that scavenging arrangements and road sweeping were to be considerably improved.

On the 19th October 1923 William Cowley retired from the chair having played a diminishing role in the affairs of the village, but at the meeting he reported that the Newhaven Rural District Council had applied for the power of the Housing and Town Planning Act to be put in force in the district. This is surprising since the Rural District Council had been giving planning approval to the houses on the Wyke and Downs estates since November 1907 or even earlier. One benefit of the Act led to the building of workmen's houses in the village. In the summer of 1924 the Council finally agreed to the Brighton Fire Brigade taking over responsibilities in the Black Rock Ward. The word "Ward" was used for the first time in the Council Minutes meaning an electoral division of the village.

There was a string of complaints during that summer, the illicit stacking of drain pipes on the village green, the dirty state of the roads, the lack of public toilets and the endless prevarication of Tillings over the cost of bus fares, lead the Parish Council to write to the District Council asking for the power to start competition in an effort to force down the cost of fares. An offer to buy a steam-driven fire engine caught their imagination but on learning that it would cost £120 the offer was refused. In October of the same year they learned of the possibility of having a new electrical supply from Brighton which would have cheered the community had they not been more interested in who were to be the lucky occupants of the new workmen's cottages in Park Place. Based on an "as needs basis" twenty names were put forward, one of which was Mr Marshall of Dunrobin, Warren Avenue, Race Hill, Nr Brighton. There was no recognition here of the name Downs or Wick Estate, but that is not surprising; Mr Cowley who had Woodendean Farm and was chairman of the Parish Council from February 1921 to October 1923, never referred to either name in meetings, or if he did it simply went unrecorded. That is also difficult to understand, but it does indicate that there was a discussion as to whether or not people living on the Downs or Wick Estate were now being considered and also that at least one family was regarded as being in greater need than the people of Rottingdean. Who put his name forward and how he became to be considered is not recorded but someone certainly did. The Parish Council were now in new territory in both senses of the word and were at last conscious of its existence.

It must be said that the Council members were a very dedicated and hard working group of people who took all the complaints on board and sorted out the problems of which there were many and varied; they worked tirelessly under a lot of pressure from a number of people in the village with insufficient community income to carry out ongoing capital works programmes or simply do the things that the village needed. They were active, timely and unstinting in their efforts to make Rottingdean a good place to live in, independent and separate from Brighton. It was their village and they were proud of their birthplace and their fierce independence. When I went to the Church of England Primary School at the foot of Neville Road with my sister in 1946 that independence was still evident and it remained that way for very many years.

In January 1925 four names were added to the list of Councillors making eleven in total and in the following April, R C V Lang was appointed Chairman. At the same time they also voted on their first woman Councillor to represent the managers of the Church of England Primary School.

Eustace and Harold join the party

Their inaugural meeting on the Parish Council was on the 14th December 1925 and the very first point on the agenda required them to vote on a proposal put forward by the Piddinghoe Parish Council to support a petition for Southern Railway to connect up the district with their railway system. Now Eustace and Harold could immediately see the benefit this would bring to the people on the Wick and Downs Estates as a further means of transport to an isolated and growing community. However, the Councillors thought differently and saw it as an intrusion, no doubt instigated by the oligarchs in the village, and so voted to "let the letter lie on the table". Eustace and Harold moved an amendment "that the Rottingdean Parish Council do give their support to the Petition" which was voted down nine votes to two. Their amendment was defeated and "the letter do lie on the table". Their defeat was a harsh reality into the politics of the Parish Council and the real masters of the village who, as long ago as 1910, demanded that the village policeman confine his duties to the village only and was not to visit the outlying areas.

It is highly improbable that anyone serving on the Committee at that time would have remembered the 1886 Parliamentary Session at which a Bill was proposed for the construction of a railway from Brighton to Newhaven that would involve the Compulsory Purchase of Land along its route, but more especially in Rottingdean where the land was owned by The Marquis of Abergavenny and occupied by Henry Cowley. The route of the railway took it along the south side of the windmill, across the High Street south of St Margaret's Church, north-eastwards to Newlands Barn, turning there down towards modern day Saltdean. Needless to say the railway never got off the ground!

Harold and Eustace were more fortunate at their next meeting in February 1926 at which it was resolved -

"That the Rural District Council be asked to officially recognise that portion of the road leading out of Rottingdean towards Falmer and which extends from the Garage at Down House to the Brown Egg Poultry Farm as Woodingdean Road".

Furthermore *"that the carrying out of the suggested temporary repairs of the Warren Road, the Rural District Council be asked to repair only a portion of the width so as not to interfere with through traffic".*

Eustace and Harold were on a roll and moved that the *"East Sussex County Council be approached with a view to the provision of a Public Elementary School in the Downs Ward of the Parish. At present there are approximately 60-70 children of school age in this district, the district is developing rapidly and attendance at school at present necessitates a journey of at least two and a half miles over very exposed country".*

At the next meeting a month later they learned that the Parish Council had heard from the Rural District Council *'that whilst they had no power to name streets in their district they will recognise that portion of road between Down House Garage and Brown Egg Poultry Farm as Woodingdean Road'.* That was to have a long and lasting effect on the future of Rottingdean. It stated that the County Borough was bringing forward proposals for the extension of its boundaries and enclosed a map showing the proposed extension to which Parliamentary sanction would be sought at the next session. The plan showed that it was proposed to absorb the whole of the Parish of Rottingdean, and it was stated that if the proposals received the sanction of Parliament the absorption would probably take place as from 1st November 1927.

The Council decided to take no action but wait for further proposals and that the matter should come before a Parish meeting in order that the feelings of the parishioners could be ascertained. That should, of course, have included those living on the Downs and Wick Estates but whether it did or not went unrecorded.

Clearly both Eustace Gibson and Harold Price had an appetite to make their voices heard and for changes to be made. Their presence on the Council may have actually upset some of the Councillors who were forced to listen and act on difficult matters arising on the northern lands of their own parish, a land hitherto completely ignored, not through any sort of malice or ignorance but simply because there was more than enough to do in Rottingdean without taking on the additional problems of the community in the north. There is no doubt that Eustace and Harold generated the energy for the sustainable improvements and for the well-being of people then living on the Downs behind Rottingdean. There was no guidance given, no prescription of how things should happen and most probably by now all the Councillors were powerless to prevent the development from quietly unfolding.

Eustace Gibson and his wife Ella lived at 'Southdown' on the Warren Road near their chemist shop at the crossroads and later they lived in Balsdean Road. Harold Price lived in The Ridgway where in 1926 he is listed as a poultry farmer. Only one other family is listed in Kelly's as living on the Downs Estate in 1926 which is incorrect. By 1936 there were 171 families living on the Downs Estate including the Falmer Road, 113 on the Wick Estate including Warren Avenue, 23 on the Farm Hill Estate, 37 on Warren Road and 31 families living elsewhere.

In June 1926 Eustace and Harold continued the fight for rights when the question of the number of fire hydrants in the Woodingdean Ward was raised and also to enquire whether the Brighton Corporation Waterworks main water supply pipe along Warren Road could be tapped in the direction of Falmer Road (above the crossroads) and also be tapped to supply water down Downs Road, along Warren Way and on to the Downs Estate where there was no mains supply. It is interesting that at this meeting in June 1926 Black Rock was also being referred to as a "Ward". At the same time it was agreed to ask the Electricity Committee of the Brighton Corporation if a supply of electricity could be carried to the Woodingdean Ward of the Parish. At the following meeting in July at which neither Eustace nor Harold were present the Clerk reported that the Brighton Electricity Works had advised *"an electricity supply could not be entertained because the possible revenue from the district would be quite inadequate to justify the expenditure"*. It was also heard that the Education Committee of the East Sussex County Council had decided to take no further action on the matter of the provision of schools' accommodation in the

Woodingdean Ward. This was to be the first time that the County Council had used the name Woodingdean Ward in addressing the Parish Council. A letter was read by the Clerk from the Hon Secretary of the Downs Labour Party asking the Parish Council to suggest an amendment to the Bye-law regarding the three mile limit of distance to and from school. It was resolved that the Education Committee be asked to take immediate action for the conveyance of the children. A political party had arrived on the scene.

The Chief Fire Officer at Brighton proved helpful by telling the Council that there were six working fire hydrants along the front of Warren Farm buildings but the main supply ended at the west entrance to the Warren Farm School and that any fire beyond that could only be dealt with by first aid measures. A letter from the Brighton Corporation Waterworks confirmed the worst that, on account of the small pressure and the restricted capacity of the pipe, it would be useless to extend it beyond the present limit of the 2inch pipe at the top of Downs Road. It was at this point on the green opposite the Downs Hotel (opened in September 1925) that the villagers collected their water in buckets or had Mr Pitteway deliver it by donkey and cart. Since the Downs Hotel was the most important building to the west of the Downs Estate it was clear that the Rock Brewery Company were advised to seriously consider extending the 4-inch pipe and fit a hydrant close at hand in the case of fire. However at the next meeting of the Council in October at which Eustace and Harold were present the Rock Brewery advised that they were only prepared to pay a proportion of the cost of extending the main based on the frontage of their property. It was then decided to leave the whole matter in abeyance hoping that the water main would be extended by the Brighton Borough Council, in other words get Brighton to pay for it. On top of that bad news the Education Committee advised the Council they would not entertain the idea of transporting the children to and from school; however, the Parish Council still felt strongly enough about the matter to request the Committee to reconsider their decision during the forthcoming winter at least.

At this meeting in October 1926 the Parish Council seemed to be showing more interest in the possibility of being absorbed into the Borough of Brighton and since the time was now right they agreed to be informed in detail as to how it affected their area, especially in regard to what was proposed in the nature of acquisition of open spaces, the extension of the water main and the electricity supply, also sea defence works at Rottingdean 'that the attitude of the Council could take shape'.

The Clerk read out a very important letter from the East Sussex County Council stating that the changing of the name of the Downs Ward to Woodingdean Ward had now been approved; however, on the downside the East Sussex Education Committee had decided to adhere to their decision not to convey children to and from school in the Woodingdean Ward.

Harold may have thought that things were very much going his way and that anything he could do for Rottingdean could only improve his chances of achieving more, so he got himself involved in designing the one-way traffic system around the village green which is still in existence to this day. At the same meeting, the Clerk said that a conference between the members of the Parish Council and representatives of the Brighton Corporation was fixed for the 21st January in the Rottingdean village hall and that the Chairman should seek clarification of a number of important points including the extension of the water and electricity mains, education of distant children, transport, sewage and road building. Eustace and Harold attended the meeting when it was resolved that all the representatives would attend a further meeting on the 9th February to hear further explanation of the Brighton Borough Extension Scheme and that a decision of the parishioners would be taken. Here we can see Eustace Gibson and Harold Price leading the people of the Woodingdean Ward towards inclusion in the grand scheme.

At a later meeting in March 1927 whereat both Eustace and Harold were present it was recorded that the Parish Council was not adverse to the proposed incorporation of the parish of Rottingdean within the boundary of the County Borough of Brighton provided that the differentiation of rating should be spread over a period of at least nine years. The resolution was passed to the East Sussex County Council and the Newhaven Rural District Council with the request that it be dealt with in the appropriate manner when the Brighton Corporation Bill was before Parliament. Not being put off by these important landmarks Harold again raised the question of the conveyance of children in the Woodingdean Ward and a month later he proposed that a letter be sent to the Brighton Town Council Watch Committee saying the matter of half-price fares for children on Messrs Tillings buses be brought forward for discussion, pointing out that Tillings already issued half-price fares in the London area. The argument with Tillings, however, rumbled on for several months with an unsatisfactory ending save that Tillings did produce an improved timetable for their services.

At the end of the Parish meeting on the 6th July 1927 Harold proposed that, in view of the proposed incorporation of the parish, the Education Committee be asked to make provision for the erection of a temporary or permanent school at Woodingdean near the Downs Hotel as no local education facilities for the children were available, except the schools at Rottingdean or Brighton both of which were over two miles distant.

This was the first time that the name 'Woodingdean' was recorded in preference to 'Woodingdean Ward'.

The meetings by now were getting shorter with the prospect that the community was about to be absorbed into Brighton, a fact that not everyone would be happy with. Rottingdean was fiercely independent albeit with little enough money to meet the high cost of coastal erosion. Village oligarchs did not become public servants at Parish level and I can only imagine their private thoughts on the prospect of joining up with Brighton. We must not, however, believe that all was well between the oligarchs because sometime earlier Steyning Beard was more interested in writing to the local paper regarding the controversy over a footpath which Mr Burne-Jones alleges he has blocked up. He also referred to previous disagreements with the Burne-Jones family regarding the subject of footpaths and the manipulation of the newly-formed parish councils to 'stir up ill feelings towards the so-called oppressors of the working man'. Strong stuff and deeply felt by those who employed farm hands by the score.

Whilst all that was going on, the community at Woodingdean would have thought differently as most had come from the Brighton area and would have been only too pleased to have the financial strength of the larger town on hand to pay for the improvements needed to create a village with modern services and roads so long denied them. Percy Harvey Estates provided nothing except the basic plot of ground, Newhaven Rural District Council saw Woodingdean as a millstone at the far end of their territory and the East Sussex County Council provided little, preferring to wait until the Incorporation was completed. Brighton Council initially provided very little until the Act was passed on the 1st April 1928 and the Rottingdean Parish Council only helped after Eustace Gibson and Harold Price joined them in December 1925, thirteen years after William Cowley had sold a large portion of his Woodendean Farm and the Downs Estate established.

The penultimate meeting of the Parish Council was held on the 16th October 1927 where it was reported that the Secretary to the Brighton Education Committee in a letter dated 8th July 1927 stated that 'a temporary or permanent school at Woodingdean would be considered'. The village had to wait until the 2nd September 1929 when the Woodingdean Temporary Council School No 42 was opened in the Church Hall, Downsway under the head teacher Mr Dutton Briant, and the first three young lads, Frank and Charles Whibley and their pal Harold Smith walked in for the very first time. See WR&TM page 43 for the story of this school.

The Brighton Education Committee had at last recognised the name Woodingdean.

Eustace Gibson served the Parish Council for nearly two years and achieved a very great deal and although he resigned at the penultimate meeting he and Harold Price should be remembered for the work they did on behalf of the community of Woodingdean, not only for getting the village on the map but also, and far more importantly, for the adoption of the name Woodingdean. Although Eustace gave much, it was probably Harold who steered the Rottingdean Parish Council to finally adopt the permanent name Woodingdean. It was not until 1952 that the final Act came about when Woodingdean was taken out of the Parish of Rottingdean to become "The District (or Parish) of the Holy Cross Woodingdean", a separate Parish in its own right.

The very last meeting of the parish Council was held on the 30th March 1928 and Harold as ever was present. As he walked away for the last time he must have reflected on the work that both he and Eustace had done to establish the separate parish of Woodingdean, for without their efforts and persistence it is very likely that things may have turned out rather differently.

The Rottingdean Parish Council meetings spanned the years from1895 to 1928 and nowhere in the minutes did the name Woodingdean appear until 1926 when the East Sussex County Council approved the name change from Downs Ward to Woodingdean Ward. Even when William Cowley sold off part of his farm to the Harvey Estates in 1913 to create the Downs Estate and again in 1919 when Robert and George Leman of London sold off part of Norton Farm to Henry Pannett to create the Wyke Estate did the name Woodingdean appear. The defining historical moments came on the 6th July 1927 when, as a result of Harold Price asking for a temporary school, the name Woodingdean was formally recorded in the Parish Council Minutes and again two days later when the Brighton Education Committee also formally again referred to the name Woodingdean.

Harold Price lived in the village for forty-one years and always took an interest in public life and was elected onto the British Legion Committee at Rottingdean in October 1933. A year later he put up as an Independent Candidate and with support from the Conservative Committee succeeded in getting himself onto the Council by just eighteen votes. In 1960 Harold and his wife Nancy retired to Cornwall where they settled and lived happily, leading much the same life they had always lived. Sadly, Harold died in 1978 and Nancy passed away in 1985. John, Alan and Maureen live in the West Country and their youngest daughter Sheila lives in Seaford, Sussex. For the story of the Price family see THMP pages 113-117.

Robert Vaughan Lang, Chairman of the Rottingdean Parish Council for so many years and former headmaster of St Aubyns School, was born on the 2nd October 1871. He first appears as a member of the Parish Council in 1908 as having arranged to fix a warning sign to motorists on Brighton Hill. He died on the 14 August 1940 and a memorial tablet in his name was authorised on the 5th November 1942. (PAR 466/4)

◄o►◄o►◄o►

The Village crossroads in times gone by

Slater's Stores, the first shop in Woodingdean, was originally owned by Elizabeth and Sarah Sleightholm around 1920 but sold out to Fred Slater in 1925 pictured here with his sister in the doorway. The Sleightholm sisters sold groceries, daily papers and afternoon teas at tables inside the shop. A young Cyril Pavey leaning on the fence assisted Fred Slater and his three sisters Gertrude, Lizzie and Mabel whose background was the entertainment business with the delivery of bread to outlying homes. Cyril passed away in the 1990s. Mr Hardiment, who stood for election on the Rottingdean Parish Council, lived in the tall house shown on The Ridgway from where he also ran a dairy further down the road.

A 1926/27 general view of the shops showing Sleightholm's now dilapidated shop to the left of Fred Slater's new whitewashed stores alongside. The shop was built by Albert Stowell who arrived at the village in about 1923. Stowell originally wanted to build shops on the opposite side of the crossroads but was refused because the site had been earmarked for the Downs Hotel in 1925. The land to the left on which the north Woodingdean estate was built was then known as the Brighton Heights Estate. Notice the hay stacks up Balsdean Road.

A similar scene a year or so later with the sign advertising land for sale on the Brighton Heights Estate. Slater's Stores has been re-roofed to provide additional accommodation and the road has now been hardened, although ploughing came up to the edge of the road. Tom and Isabella Newbury's Tea Rooms which he made into the Downland Cabaret Dance Club is open for business alongside Ernest and Elizabeth Goodenough's Post office. Ernest was decorated during the First World War with the Military Medal and became the first Postmaster in the village. Their two sons Robin and Sydney live in The Ridgway.

View from the cinder path in about 1928 showing Harold Price's garage under construction, Robinson's Stores completed and the new Sports Hall or Village Hall at the top of The Ridgway from where the Woodingdean Football club and the Downs Cricket Club were first established in 1926. Notice the large plots of ground between Falmer Road and The Ridgway.

A general view a year or so later with the garage now selling petrol. Mr Elkington's photography shop is next door. For a while the shop was owned by Mr and Mrs Fewel who had it as a fish and chip shop where Max Miller the comedian often stopped on his way home to Woodingdean House at Woodendean. Later on the shop was owned by Laurie Ridd, an electrical engineer.

Albert Stowell's Emporium built by himself out of two old army huts in 1923. Albert sold nearly everything from the store including second-hand furniture, particularly popular at the time to cash strapped families during the 1920s, he also acted as a land agent. Albert had been a roustabout in America where he married Grace Dunk. Their children Albert, Grace, Kenneth, Ernest, Agnes, Elsie and Alvilde were all raised in the village. Elsie periodically comes over from America to the place she loves. Alvilde Stowell, Margaret Robinson and Sydney Goodenough pose for the cameraman during the late 1930s. Tom Newbury bought the premises and turned it into a Dance Hall and after the war Fanny Palmer took it over and turned it into a fish and chip shop selling bags of chips for 2d. See THMP pages 118 - 121 for the story of the Stowell family.

Robinson's Stores under construction by Albert Stowell in the mid-1920s before Mr Robinson took it over in 1931. Mr Stowell and his family lived here for a while and continued to sell second-hand furniture. Here he is selling a splendid flock mattress for 10/- (50p), a fine washing machine for 25/- and amongst other things a cupboard for 5/-.

A mid-1930s view down Falmer Road before the road was widened and made up with pavements. Mr Goodenough's Post Office also sold household products and bowls it would seem were popular! Mr Stowell still traded second-hand furniture from next door.

Mr Robinson advertises the opening of his General Stores in about 1931. Mr Stowell's van sits outside. The post office is to the left.

Frank and Florence or Florrie Robinson at their Golden Wedding Anniversary in 1970. Frank was born in 1897 and with Florrie came to Woodingdean in 1926/27 to live in Crescent Drive where he had an acre of ground on which he kept pigs and poultry which were close to his heart. Frank and his father were partners in a Corn Merchant's business in Preston Drove, Brighton and Frank toured the area as a young man selling poultry food particularly in Woodingdean which had plenty of poultry farms. With his knowledge of running a shop Frank and Florrie decided in 1931 to start a grocer's shop in Falmer Road, a shop not long built by Albert Stowell who was living there at the time. From the start business was fairly brisk, albeit the population of the village was still quite small; however, as they were one of the only two grocers on the Downs Estate and certainly the only poultry food stockists in the village business soon picked up. Later they took on Ida Brown and Florence Hay as staff and on occasions when they were extra busy their son Ray and daughter Margaret helped out.

Tom Newbury's Downland Cabaret Dance Club, Goodenough's Post Office and Robinson's Stores in the late 1920s.

Alice Chapman's tea shop, tobacconist and confectionery shop in about 1927. Alice had the first private library in the village and charged a 1d a week but titles were very limited. Mr Chapman was blind and attended St Dunstans at Ovingdean.

Mrs Chapman's when there were no houses in The Ridgway. The Café passed through a number of hands ending up with John Pope who changed its name to 'Joy's Café' after his wife. Mr Pope kept my sweet coupons for several years whilst sweets were on ration. What a delight to get 2ozs of chocolate!

Thomas Tilling's service 2B dropped off their passengers to take a ramble in the countryside and also take tea at Mrs Chapman's. Here we see passengers making their way to her Café.

An 'uphill' shot in about 1929 before the Falmer Road was made up. The spare plot of ground being offered for sale between Chapmans and Ridds would have cost about £40. A sign at the top of the picture offers plot lands for sale for £35 each. Where is everbody?

An opposite view possibly about the same time. The original roof on Slater's Stores has been altered and the bushes to the left hide the remains of Edith Sleightholm's first village shop.

Downs Road in about 1928 with one sign advertising the land on the Downs Estate and the other the land on Brighton Heights Estate. The Downs Hotel opened in September 1925 but also served tea in the garden which quietly changed into the car park over the years. Notice the narrow width of Downs Road. Mr Stowell's van can be seen outside his second-hand furniture shop.

A similar view but a few years later after the speed limit signs had been put up. Notice how close they are to the cross-roads. The Brighton Heights Estate sign is still up but like all signs it was removed during the war.

The crossroads showing the public water point that served the village until 1929 when services were eventually laid. The photograph was taken before Mrs Newbury's Happy Corner café was built in the mid-1930s. Mrs Wood's fruit Stores and 'Australia', a weather-boarded building is shown. Just in front of the Downs Estate sign can be seen the only signpost for the 'Downs Road'. Harold Price's first garage can be seen in the background above the Fruit Stores sign.

By 1935 the parade of shops has matured, the cut road is in and the new pavement laid down the Falmer Road offers a young Robin Goodenough a smooth surface on which to run his hand cart outside his father's Post Office. Mr Stowell has finished with his Emporium and now deals with electrical items and has opened an Estate Office calling himself 'Business Transfer Agents'. He is now selling both bungalows and plots on the Downs Estate and his new black car is a sign of his success. A postbox and the iconic ice-cream cone has appeared which was to remain outside Slater's Stores for many years.

Robin Goodenough in 2010 still resides with his brother Syd in the village.

Gordon Newbury parking his bike outside the family-run Happy Corner Café from where Gordon ran his other business that of a house painter and decorator. The store sold general confectionery, hot tea to the passers-by and had a large room where they ran dances and held parties and dinners for the Downs Cricket Club, which I particularly remember as a youngster for it was here that I developed my lifelong love of the sport. The photograph was probably taken in the early 1950s and shows the open Brighton Heights Estate a few years before being swallowed up for the north Woodingdean Estate. Notice the 220-feet-long plots of land up Balsdean Road where, on their northern boundary, would have run a new road called Wick Avenue had Oscar Selbach's estate gone ahead to fruition. Gordon and Marion Newbury were well known and respected in the village. They were the 'centre' of the village for very many years and their daughter Lynette still lives there with her family.

A lovely view across Balsdean Road. It was later to be renamed Warren Way when the Brighton Heights Estate didn't materialize. Mr Yeatman's Laundry is already in place and his barber's shop is still there today. Notice again the large plots of ground purchased by some of the more wealthy pioneers.

A chalky white Warren Way and Balsdean Road in the mid-1920s.

A reverse view a year or so later. Mr Yeatman's Laundry has arrived.

Looking across the Brighton Heights Estate towards The Ridgway.

The village crossroads in 1937 showing the Police Box and the only public telephone box in the village. A lovely view of the Brighton Heights Estate which was to become the north Woodingdean Housing Estate twenty years later.

An immediate postwar view of the Downs Hotel with the flat-roofed prefab bungalows opposite the Church whose cross stands very proudly above the trees. The village was still traffic free and the Hotel car park was open to all. The Downs Hotel was originally owned by the Rock Brewery Brighton Ltd which specialised in draught and bottled beers in 'excellent condition'. 'Try a small Rock' was their sales slogan. They boasted 'ten well-furnished bedrooms, a coffee room for fifty people, a lounge and a saloon bar with excellent water and sanitary arrangements and all bedrooms fitted with hot and cold water lavatory basins'. For the rider they could offer a riding stable within five minutes walk where hacks and hunters could be hired as required and for those with a sedentary inclination a half-acre tea garden beckoned alongside the hotel. Luncheons, teas and dinners were served at short notice at popular prices. The general tariff read, bed and breakfast 8s-6d, daily accommodation 15s - 0d, or £4 - 4s - 0d a week. For weekenders, Friday dinner to Monday breakfast was £2 - 2s - 0d. To assist the motorist they offered parking for forty cars in a private road or if visitors preferred they could be collected at Brighton Station for three shillings and six pence (17$\frac{1}{2}$p!). Mr Price took the opportunity to advertise his garage in the promotional booklet about the Hotel by offering the visitor any journey at 9d per mile plus any waiting time at 2s - 6d an hour. Cars could be garaged there at 1s - 0d a night or 4s - 6d a week, motorcycle solos charged half-price. Not wishing to lose any opportunity for business, Mr Price also advertised his 'Brighton Downs Motor Services' which ran two services; Service No 1, a half-hour bus service to the top of Elm Grove for 3d and Service No 2, a two-hourly service to Rottingdean for 4d. It read that 'any suggestions or complaints respecting the service should be addressed in writing to the Secretary Mr Harold Price'. Lovely days! Thrower and Woolgar, the family butchers, advertised in the booklet telling the customer of daily supplies of lamb from Canterbury. Mr Slater also advertised, as did Mr Parker the first owner of a tea room in the village, even preceding Mrs Chapman just below the crossroads.

The crossroads in the 1920s. The land on which the Downs Hotel was built upon was owned by Charlie Tarrent who had a pig farm there before 1920.

Harold Price's Woodingdean Garage in the late 1920s with Ernie Souch a local carrier watching a delivery of petrol destined for use by the few car owners in the village.

Price's Woodingdean Garage, purchased by Bill Sheaff from Harry Coe in February 1950 for a reputed sum of £3,000. Petrol rationing ended in May 1950 and cost 2s 9d (14p) a gallon. Mr Sheaff had a hunch that the garage could be developed into a modern efficient garage with showrooms and petrol sales that would rise from 10,800 gallons to 100,000 gallons a year by 1958.

The garage four months later in April 1950. Same building and "Shell" pumps but now painted up.

Within two years Bill Sheaff had demolished the village garage that had stood for thirty years and erected his new modern premises flanked on either side by two original shops- Robinson's Stores and Laurie Ridd's electrical shop. Wally Chapman stands alongside Ernie Brazier's low-loader waiting to be filled up. The garage was built by Bill Martin, one of several village builders.

In 1956 only three of the original shops remained - Robinson's Stores and Joy's Café, formerly Mrs Chapman's tea Shop, and Slater's Stores, out of picture. It was close to this spot that actor Errol Flynn's mother was killed by a bubble car in 1966. Errol's parents, Marelle and Professor Theodore Flynn lived for a while in McWilliam Road where the actor occasionally visited them.

In the early 1960s the circle was almost complete. Joy's Café remained, but somewhat altered, and only Slater's Stores the third shop in Woodingdean remains intact. The District Bank had arrived only to be taken over by the National Westminster Bank some years later.

The garage and crossroads in January 1963 when the village was cut off and facing the worst winter in living memory.

Mr Yeatman's Laundry was an imposing building. The backs of Slater's Stores and Stowell's Emporium can be seen as well as Sam Woolgar's butcher's shop in the distance. The photograph was taken before 1928 as the Church Hall in Downsway is yet to be built.

Chris Yeatman inherited the business from his father and still carries on as the local barber, a tradition extending over eighty years by the same family. The photograph, taken in 2010 shows the original entrance doors to his shop. Walter Yeatman and his two sisters, Miriam and Rhoda, came to Woodingdean with their mother Vera in about 1922 from Redhill where the family had a barber's shop and where young Walter learned his trade. After looking around the area they purchased a plot of ground on the Downs Estate and on it they built their present shop from two unwanted sectional buildings from Shoreham Airport. With a growing community on their doorstep they started a laundry which soon took off and became very busy. Walter, or "Wally" as he was always known, drove the delivery van, but as people found out that he was a barber they encouraged him to set up the shop which to this day is still running. Just after the war a ladies' hairdressers was added.

The pilot of this biplane said he 'fancied a drink' and landed in Oscar Selbach's field opposite the Downs Hotel. The pilot's name is lost in time but the little boy minding the plane is McClennon Cuthbertson aged about six. The gentleman with him is not recognised but we know that Duncan Cuthbertson his father took the photograph. Notice the crowd of people outside the Downs Hotel; were they there for the opening of the Hotel in September 1925 or were they just a crowd waiting for the Tilling's bus?

Alvilde and Elsie (standing) Stowell at an 'English Tea' in California where they lived most of their lives. Photograph taken in 2002. The family lived in Occupation Road, most probably chosen for its quiet location and large plots of ground.

We become a new Parish

During the period when the Downs and Wick Estates were created and the village formed it lay within the parish of Rottingdean and remained so until 1952 when Woodingdean was made a separate parish in its own right.

The majority of medieval parishes were formed by 1200 and some had been in existence for hundreds of years. According to David Hey, from the 9th century onwards local lords founded churches to serve their estates, the boundaries of which were naturally used as the boundaries of the new parishes which sometimes caused disputes if the ministers were not consulted. A parish was not only a unit of pastoral care, but one that was expected to provide the resources to maintain its church and support its priest, thus causing disputes centred upon the payment of tithes and offerings etc. Burial rights were jealously guarded by the incumbents of churches who were watchful over the claims of new chapels-of-ease. There was a natural tendency for parishes to follow convenient existing boundaries, some of which were ancient, many preserving the outline of pre-conquest estates. The traditional definition is 'that circuit of ground which is committed to the charge of one person or vicar, or to another minister having cure for the souls therein'. Or 'The parish is the territorial basis of community service'. a view long held by the great Archbishop of Canterbury, Theodore of Tarsus. According to the distinguished historian Bryant 'the cradle of our liberties was the village'.

Centuries before universal suffrage was ever dreamt of we were governing ourselves; the local community was the only real authority; the parish was the unit of government. Every householder had to serve his year as an unpaid administrator of the nation's business; certainly, reluctantly, he had to take his turn in one of the parish offices whilst the mantle of authority rested on his humble and unlettered shoulders. Sometimes they were good and sometimes bad but he learnt a good deal and at the end of his year he went back into the general body of the village community with what he had learnt. He transmitted it to his children. W E Tate; The Parish Chest, Phillimore & Co Ltd 1983.

A cautious approach is needed to determine how the parish of Rottingdean was formed, as a landholding was always in a state of transition. The shape of a parish varied from one part of the country to another and was strongly influenced by variations of soil within the parish and size was often determined by population levels. The Local Government Act 1894 divided England and Wales into some 14,000 parishes, whose boundaries generally followed those of old civil parishes. Anomalies caused by divided parishes and detached portions were removed. Elected Parish Councils which were formed, such as Rottingdean in 1895 survived the reorganisation of local government in 1974.

The Church of the Holy Cross, only the lych-gate now remains of the original church. The original red brick boundary walls were demolished and replaced by the Thakeham block walls in the 1950s. This postcard was posted to Cambridge on the 10th October 1958.

The map of the District of Holy Cross of Woodingdean in 1952 shows the conventional District on the north side running along the hedgerow south of Drove Road which is actually in the parish of Falmer. In the same year Wick Farm, situated west of the Warren Farm Schools, changed its name to Warren Farm and Wick Farm located east of the top of Falmer Road. The conventional District follows the exact line of the northern part of the Parish of Rottingdean; however, a small area of the Parish of Rottingdean bounded by Overhill Road on the south side and the ancient woodland boundary to the west, Falmer Road to the east intersecting at the junction of Occupation Road and Falmer road was transferred to the Parish of Ovingdean. At the same time an area of the Parish of Ovingdean bounded in the north by an extension of the line of a fence at the bottom of Falmer Road, a line on the eastern side and a line following the centre of the Falmer Road on the western side down to where they intersect at the end of Occupation Road was transferred from the Parish of Ovingdean to the Parish of Rottingdean. What is clear is that people living in that area at the bottom of Falmer Road down to Occupation Road had lived in the Parish of Ovingdean until the transfer in 1952. See map 14. The areas in question affected where people voted.

In 1929 there were 550 voters in Rottingdean Ward East (Polling District T4), effectively Woodingdean including 23 residents of Warren Farm School plus a further 11 living at Balsdean named as
John and Rebecca Kincaide in Balsdean Cottage
Agnes Sneddon also in Balsdean Cottage
Mary, Alfred and Charles Jones in Norton Cottage
Charles and Ellen Knight in Norton Bungalow
Guy and Nora Woodman and Ethel Amelia Cramp in Balsdean Manor House.

By 1931 and 1933 the number of voters in the same ward had risen to 652 and 791 respectively.

In 1946 a small area of south Woodingdean lay in the parliamentary Constituency of Lewes but the registration unit was part of the Parish of Brighton Rottingdean Ward (Central). The Parliamentary Polling District was Rottingdean Central (V) and the Local Government Polling District was Rottingdean Central T4 which necessitated 13 people to vote in the Rottingdean Central areas. The remaining 1517 voters in the greater area of Woodingdean which lay in the same Lewes division but in the Rottingdean Ward (East) voted in the Rottingdean East Ward and Rottingdean East T5 Wards. There were a further 37 voters listed in the Service Register required to vote in the latter. All rather unnecessarily complicated.

By 1948 there were 20 voters out of a total of 2061 still having to vote in Rottingdean Central V and T4. At the time of the parish boundary change in 1952 there were still 22 voters marooned in Crescent Drive South and Falmer Road in the Rottingdean Central Ward whilst the remaining 2310 voters all still voted in the Local Government Polling District of Rottingdean East. This situation was rectified in 1953 when the few voters in Crescent Drive South and Falmer Road were absorbed into Warren Ward (East) and all 2340 on the roll voted together.

There had been a steady growth in the population of Woodingdean up until the early 1950s after which the population really took off due in the main to the building of the South and North Woodingdean estates. This affected the number in the congregation attending the Church of the Holy Cross which had only been in existence for a few short years but was already showing signs of structural failure. Before its existence the village had no church, only a church hall and before that a green-painted mission hall at the bottom of Downs Road. The full history of the coming of the mission hall and the Church are recorded in WR&TM but it is well to briefly remind ourselves of what happened as it played a minor part in the creation of the new Parish.

It was not until the nuns took up residence at the newly built St Mary's Home in Rottingdean in 1911 that Sunday School actually started in the homes of the children on the Wick and Downs Estates. The slowly growing population then began to look for some sort of permanent building or mission in which they could gather under one roof for services as well as Sunday School. That mission hall was provided by Mr and Mrs Harry Pitt in 1918 shortly after their arrival in the village from Yorkshire. Mr and Mrs Pitt purchased Philip Bailey's bungalow on the brow overlooking Downs Road which could only then be approached by a long slippery path up the side of the hill. It is worth mentioning that Mr Bailey was one of the very first, if not the first person to take up occupation on the Downs Estate.

A historically priceless painting of the Mission Hall by Douglas Holland with the Pitt's bungalow behind on the hill in the early days there were about forty parishioners.

The altar in the Mission Hall at Harvest Thanksgiving in the 1920s. There was a trap door in the floor through which mischievous children could escape to play in the void below. At Christmas time the crib usually contained a real live baby Jesus and on one occasion it was very young Robin Goodenough who still lives in the village. This is the only known photograph of the inside of the Hall and was contributed by Robin.

Harry and Alice Pitt became aware that there was no place of worship and so suggested that they set up a surplus army hut on their property alongside the Downs Road which in those days was no more than a track. The hut was consecrated and became the Mission Church with Mr Pitt as Churchwarden and Mrs Pitt the organist. Services were taken on Sunday morning and evenings by Mr Kerr, a lay preacher from Rottingdean and, later, in 1923, by a Church Army Evangelist David Powell. He was succeeded by another Evangelist Captain Squires who by this time presided over a congregation of about forty. The Mission had an altar but no bell to call the flock and its popularity meant that it was fast becoming too small, so an extension was added in 1922. Social activities at the Mission and in the Pitt's bungalow became very popular, particularly as no other facility of its kind existed at the time and it was a very long way to walk into Brighton. Rottingdean we remember had no similar facilities and had been urged by the East Sussex County Council to do something for its residents.

In 1926 the Chichester Diocesan Society bought a site on Warren Road large enough to accommodate a new church, a vicarage and a church hall but without funds little progress was made. With the Mission Church in a state of disrepair and with a leaking roof it was considered impracticable to relocate the Mission on the new site, besides which the newly formed troops of Boy Scouts and Girl Guides were now using the building and were eventually to take it over in 1928. When eventually the building was taken down in the 1940s the old foundations were to remain among the elderberry trees for many years. The ruins provided a place for us youngsters to climb on and to make camps in the surrounding bushes well out of sight of the bungalow high on the hill above.

A gift of £500 coupled with a grant of £100 from the Chichester Board of Finance and the appointment of Woodingdean's first resident vicar, the Rev CJ McGregor, ensured sufficient impetus for a new church hall to be started by May 1928 and finished in July of the same year. The new hall served as a church and, in the following year, as a

Opening of the Church Hall in Downsway in 1928. Many of the children were from the Warren Farm School. A very young Douglas Holland far right looks away from the camera.

Temporary Council School No 42, (see WR&TM pages 43 and 44,) thereafter the hall was used for ecclesiastical purposes only. The hall was the centre of village activities with popular summer fetes and socials, dancing and music. Everyone attended these functions and children were especially catered for. The Summer Fete of 1929 realised £40. One of the main attractions was a chauffeur and car provided by Harold Price for rides to Falmer and back! On another occasion they went on a "mystery drive" through Falmer and Lewes to the old fashioned village of Glynde, then on to Litlington where the char-a-banc "rested" whilst they made coffee over an open fire. Mr McGregor found the strain all too much and on medical advice had to give up work and go away for a month to recuperate. After 1932, Woodingdean is never mentioned again in the Rottingdean Parish Magazine and Mr McGregor's monthly letter ceased.

An inside view of the Church Hall in the 1930s

The Bishop of Chichester, Dr G K Bell, was not satisfied with the temporary arrangements for church services and advised Lewis Varey, Vicar of Rottingdean, of his intention to create a separate conventional district of Woodingdean from 1st

January 1933, thus all connection between the Parish of Rottingdean and the Woodingdean Mission District would cease. The district would then become to all intents and purposes a separate Parish with a Priest in Charge responsible directly to the Bishop of the Diocese. Rev McGregor, quite rightfully after all his dedication, became the first Priest in Charge.

The Church of the Holy Cross choir in the 1940s.
Back row left to right; unknown, Michael Golding, unknown, Ivor Levett holding staff, Bobby George, Bobby Faulkner, ? Bartlett, Michael Wilding. Centre row; unknown, Margery Payne, Pat Russell, John Ireland, Rev Whittle, Ivy Cullen organist and choirmistress, Kathleen Lamper, Jean Ferriman, daughter of Mr Ferriman, Superintendent of Warren Farm Industrial School. Front row; unknown, unknown, twins David and Michael Lamper who emigrated to South Africa.

In 1932 the Rev McGregor was in consultation with the Secretary of the Sussex Church Building Fund over the question of a new church. The Woodingdean Permanent Chancel Fund was inaugurated to raise the required £1,000 with the remaining £2,000 to come out of the Sussex Fund. Fundraising continued during the late 1930s with people being asked to donate a pound for a brick to build the long-awaited church. In 1940 the Rev. Arthur E Whittle succeeded Rev McGregor to become the first vicar. The church was completed in 1941 and dedicated by Bishop Bell on the 28th February, the ceremony having to be finished by 6pm when the blackout started. The lofty Holy Cross on the front gable had been sponsored by the people of Clarkville, Tennessee. The Brighton and Hove Herald reported that the building cost only £2,000 to build and was capable of seating only one hundred and fifty parishioners. The lych gate provided seats for the elderly to sit and enjoy the magnificent views of the Downs and sea and is the only part of the original buildings remaining. The first church organist quite fittingly was Sister Mable from St Mary's Home but unfortunately she developed ill health and soon retired.

Within a few years it became very evident that the little red brick church was too small for the ever-growing population and as it had developed structural faults, including a large crack in the main arch above the nave, plans were made for its replacement in September 1968. The success of our little church was there for all to see and it was partly this success that had led the Right Reverend George, Bishop of Chichester, to give his consent fourteen years earlier to the Scheme that the boundaries of the parishes of Rottingdean and Ovingdean be altered to create a new District or Parish of the Church of the Holy Cross

The Reverend Michael and Mary Finch and family in the garden of the new vicarage in 1957.

Woodingdean.

The New Parishes Measure 1943 (No1) is one of the many Measures of the Church Assembly and the General Synod of the Church of England enacted from 1920 to 1986 passed by the National Assembly of the Church of England, in order to repeal some provisions of the Church Building Acts 1818 to 1884 and authorise the formation of new ecclesiastical districts or, those as are obsolete, and to re-enact with amendments other provisions of the last Acts. The General Provisions cover the Power of Commissioners to acquire land for churches and amongst other things the provisions as to burial ground common to two or more districts and also to enable the Commissioners to declare land outside the district acquired as burial ground to be part of the district.

The Episcopal Endowments and Stipends Measure 1943 (No2) was passed by the National Assembly of the Church of

The Reverend & Mrs Richard Bromfield. Richard and his wife Jennifer moved with their daughter Sarah from the parish of St Symphorians in Durrington, West Worthing. They have lived in Sussex for the past thirty-seven years and Richard is the eighth incumbent but seventh vicar of the Holy Cross Church. Richard studied theology at what was the oldest Catholic College in the Church of England at Chichester, and holds a Masters Degree in Religious Education from Sussex University. In addition to his duties as vicar he is also Chichester Archdeaconry Warden of Readers involved in the selection and training of candidates for lay ministry in the Diocese of Chichester. Jenny works within the NHS at the Health Sciences Library at Worthing and Sarah teaches Science at a school in Worthing. They love the Sussex countryside and the Sussex coastline and hope to remain in the county when they retire in a few years time.

England to make provision for empowering the Ecclesiastical Commissioners to take over the endowments and property of any see, to pay to the bishop of the diocese an appropriate stipend to provide for him a suitable residence, to accept responsibility in respect of certain stipends and other official expenses and to deal with any existing house of residence belonging to the see. It was a condition that the bishop, who at the date of the passing of the Measure was in occupation of the see, remained in occupation.

On the 25th June 1952 the Principal Officer of the Church Commissioners in Westminster, LN King Esq. wrote to the incumbent of the benefice of Ovingdean (and most probably Rottingdean) the Reverend HJ Adams setting out the proposal under the New Parish Measure1943 saying -

'in accordance with the requirements of the New Parishes Measure 1943 I send to you as the incumbent of the benefice of Ovingdean the enclosed draft of a scheme (together with a plan thereto) prepared by the Church Commissioners in pursuance of the Measure to which they propose to submit to HM in Council for altering the boundaries of the parishes of Rottingdean and Ovingdean and for the constituting a separate district for spiritual purposes (and ultimately a new parish) to be called "The District (or Parish) of Holy Cross Woodingdean" and to be taken out of the parishes of Rottingdean and Ovingdean. I hereby give you notice that any objection to the draft Scheme be made in writing to the Commissioners within 6 weeks'.

The Church Commissioners acting in pursuance of the New Parishes Measure of 1943 laid before the Queen's Most Excellent Majesty in Council a scheme for altering the boundaries of the parishes of Rottingdean and Ovingdean in the diocese of Chichester and for constituting a new parish to be taken out of the two parishes. Simultaneously Mr King lodged the draft of the scheme with the Queen's Most Excellent Majesty in Council with the statement that -

'The area of the district or parish was defined, that is, all the contiguous parts of the parishes of Rottingdean and Ovingdean which taken together are bounded upon the east and part of the north by the parish of Kingston with Iford, upon the remaining part of the north by the parish of Falmer and upon the remaining sides by an imaginary line commencing at the point where the parish of Rottingdean, Ovingdean and Falmer meet and continuing thence first southeastwards and then generally eastwards along the boundary which divides the parish of Rottingdean from the parish of Ovingdean to a point in the middle of Falmer Road opposite the eastern end of the wall or fence which divides close numbered 8 on the map annexed hereto from close number 31- and continuing thence first southwards then southeastwards, and then southwards again along the middle of Falmer Road (thereby crossing the boundary which divides the parish of Ovingdean from the parish of Rottingdean) to a point on the boundary which divides the parish of Rottingdean from the parish of Ovingdean opposite the middle of the eastern end of Ovingdean Road, and continuing thence first northeastwards then southwards and then generally eastwards along the last-mentioned boundary to the point where it becomes most nearly contiguous to the boundary which divides the parish of Rottingdean from the parish of Kingston with Iford and continuing thence in a straight line to the nearest point on the last mentioned boundary'.

The Common Seal of the Church Commissioners was witnessed.

The Commissioners had not approved any consecrated church within the area and recommended the Bishop of Chichester accept a proposal that as from the date of the publication in the London Gazette of any Order confirming the Scheme the boundaries of the two parishes be altered in the manner proposed. Also, that as from the date of the licence of the Minister the area on the map be made a separate district for spiritual purposes. Furthermore, as from the date of consecration of a church within the area approved by the Commissioners as suitable to be a parish church or, if the church was consecrated before the approval or date of approval, the area would become a parish. The name of the district or parish as the case may be would then be 'The District or Parish of the Holy Cross Woodingdean'. in the Archdeaconry of Lewes and in the rural deanery of Brighton.

The whole reason for this act was that the spiritual interests of the area would best be served by constituting it a new parish and that a suitable endowment therefore would be provided. It is curious that they go on to say that they had not approved any consecrated church within the area (Church of the Holy Cross completed in 1941 and dedicated by Bishop Bell on the 28th February) as suitable to be the parish church of the new parish. Whether this was because the church was too small or was already showing signs of structural deterioration or a combination of other factors is not clear. The life of the little red brick church came slowly to an end during the mid-1960s but during the transition period between the old and new the services continued in the Community Centre and the Church of the Resurrection until that building was sold. The new Church of the Holy Cross was started in 1967 and dedicated by

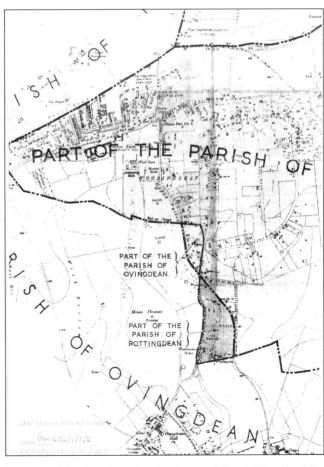

The area of the Parish of Woodingdean redefined. (Map No. 14)

The Church of The Holy Cross with the original lych gate. Photograph by Dave Billings in 2000.

the Right Reverend R P Wilson DD, Lord Bishop of Chichester, and the Vicar the Reverend Rex D T Paterson, Vicar's Warden Mr S F Warne and the People's Warden Mr A Bush during the evening of 30th September 1968. Eight young choir boys and girls awaited the service and every pew was occupied.

Incumbents of the Parish of Woodingdean.

The Reverend C J McGregor 1927 - 1940. Came to Rottingdean as part of the Mission to the Wick District Team. In 1933 Woodingdean was separated into a conventional ecclesiastical district with Mr McGregor as Priest in Charge.

The Reverend A E Whittle 1940 - 1953. The first Church of the Holy Cross was dedicated in 1941 and Mr Whittle its first 'Vicar'.

The Reverend M L Williams 1954 - 1956. Died in office.

The Reverend M Finch 1956 - 1961. Opened the daughter Church in South Woodingdean in 1959 - The Church of the Resurrection.

The Reverend R Patterson 1962 - 1973. Rebuilding of the Church of the Holy Cross - reopened in 1968. The Church of the Resurrection became St. Patrick's Catholic Church.

The Reverend R E Chatwin 1974 - 1983. Church of the Holy Cross extended.

The Reverend B Carter 1985 - 1995. Woodingdean's parish boundaries were defined and Holy Cross became the Parish Church. He was the first Vicar of the benefice.

The Reverend R Bromfield 1995 - Inducted as Vicar of the Benefice of Woodingdean. The Sanctuary was refurbished and the New Liturgy introduced. Holy Cross Window was installed.

―◁○▷―◁○▷―◁○▷―

People and Places

Early Settlers

Unfortunately space does not permit me to write about everyone that I would like to in this chapter so I have selected a few families that were among the very early settlers in the village that will be of interest to the historian and casual reader. Most of the early settlers had an interesting tale to tell but many of those are now gone leaving their families to recall their childhood lives on both estates before roads were laid and transport came to the village. Those on the Downs Estate undoubtedly had a harder time of it because of the distances involved and the fact that generally the roads were not laid until after those on the Wick Estate. However, growth in population of the two estates was very similar but those on the Wick had the advantage of being closer to the few shops and the schools and were the first to have running water. Also, they were very much closer to either the infrequent bus service to the top of Elm Grove or a walk into Brighton which a number did every day come rain or shine. According to Pike's Street Directory only six families lived in the village in 1917, which I know is incorrect; however, there were precious few others.

Drawn by the low cost of land and a beautiful downland setting a number of soldiers demobbed from the Great War saw it as a haven and were pleased for the chance to start a new life in a place of their own after the horrors of the war. Some came from Brighton as they do now, many came from London, some from further afield and a few from as far as South Africa, India and America.

Prior to the building of the Warren Farm Industrial School in the middle of the 19th century there were only three barns and one farmhouse and even after the school was built only one bungalow existed in 1899 at the foot of Warren Hill belonging to the Pavey family. Although this bungalow was extended several times it was demolished in 1940 when the family decided to build a new and more modern home on the same site.(See THMP photo No 60) After the Pavey's bungalow came the four Warren Farm Cottages in 1906 built to the plans of Edward Wright for the Guardians of the Poor of the Parish of Brighton. Planning approval was granted by the Newhaven Rural District Council on the 6th February 1906. The houses were solidly built for the staff of the School and the school's own farm and offered good accommodation for the time. All had a rear yard and cesspool drainage but only the two cottages on Old Parish Lane now remain, the other two fronting Warren Road were demolished in the 1950s for road widening. A swimming pool for the orphans of the School was built behind the two on Old Parish Lane but was demolished to make way for the junior school in 1946.

The first Planning application on the Wick Estate was made in 1907 by Architects Howard and Lavaide of Bedford Row, London for twelve elegant houses on fifty-foot-wide plots opposite the Warren Farm School for Mr C Grimwood. These houses were very different to those that followed in later years and as the drawing shows their long rear gardens extended half way up to Drove Road. The address was given as the Downs Estate which could have been an unofficial title before the Wick Estate came into being in 1919 and so it could be that both estates were to be called the Downs Estate in 1907. The houses were in the Georgian style, undoubtedly impressive and in fact superior to anything being built in either Rottingdean or Ovingdean at the time. Each had three reception rooms, a kitchen and four bedrooms and a bathroom on the first floor connected to a more expensive underground cesspool drainage system. Planning permission was granted within a fortnight but these grand houses were never built, if they had been then a very different standard would have been set for others to follow and, because of the plot sizes, they may have prevented the land around Midway Road from being developed. See figure1.

Elevation of the luxury houses for Mr Grimwood in 1907. Fig. 1.

By way of contrast Mr Johnson obtained approval for his bungalow in Valley Road after the Great War in 1921 when England was on its knees and in a desperate state, a state that dictated every aspect of our economic and social well-being. Land prices were already low but during the following decade throughout the depression of the 1920s land prices fell even further. At one point land was almost "given" away in order to survive. Mr Johnson's bungalow consisted of only a single bedroom, a kitchen with an open fire and a parlour. There was no bathroom, only an earth closet forty-five feet from the building; however, the bungalow was sited on an eight-acre plot.

During the same year William Raison commissioned Architect and Surveyor Jas. A Avery-Fowler LSA in Lewes to draw up plans for a simple bungalow in Warren Road, Race Hill for himself and family. Here we have a case of uncertain location although Warren Road was often called the Race Hill as we shall see with another Planning application. The location of his site was opposite the Warren Farm School and his plot extended up to Drove Road before Rosebury Avenue was laid, in fact in the same position of Mr Grimwood's proposal fourteen years earlier which he called the Downs Estate. Mr Raison's bungalow was a little larger than Mr Johnson's with three bedrooms and a wash room complete with a concrete floor and a copper. Although no bathroom was considered necessary they did plan to have a single earth closet fifteen feet from the building with cesspool drainage unusually located in the front garden. There are no existing buildings shown on the Architect's block plan of the whole of the Wick Estate except for Henry Hylden's slaughterhouse alongside Drove Road. Mr Raison's bungalow was approved by the Newhaven District Council in May 1921. See figure 2.

In 1922 a Planning submission was made to erect a new four-bedroom timber-framed bungalow for a smallholding at Heath Hill Farm, Race Hill, Brighton for F Ledouthet Esq of Brighton. His application was approved in May 1922.

William Raison's bungalow in 1921; neat and simple and much loved by a young family after the Great War. Fig. 2.

A year later in 1923 Mr E Ward, a Brighton Architect, applied for Planning permission to build a bungalow for his daughter Rose Ward on plot 4 of the Race Hill, again opposite Warren Farm School. Although the application was approved the bungalow was probably never built.

The largest and most ambitious development on the Race Hill in 1923 was made by Mr F M Vernon Chandon, a rather eccentric Frenchman, who gave his profession as Architect and his address as Queens Park Road, Brighton although he actually lived at 10, Race Hill. Chandon was an entrepreneur for it is said that he traded in almost anything but was apprehended by the French Military on one of his occasional return visits to France. Chandon did not own the land listed as plots 14, 16, 18 and 20 Race Hill (where the Esso Filling Station is) which he proposed to develop. His ambitious proposal was to construct a two-storey terraced building comprising a Drapers Store, Corn Merchants, an Arcade called Wick Arcade, a Butchers (most probably for Messrs Thrower and Woolgar) and a garage called Race Hill Garage with four-first floor flats above the shops under a flat corrugated iron roof with a parapet wall along the front elevation. The arcade ran between the corn merchant and the butchers to provide access to the rear of the property and to four earth closet toilets behind the corn merchants. A second development plan shows the same four toilets connected to a cesspool. The site was generous enough with a depth of 110 feet at the west end but considerably narrower, only 42 feet at the east end, where the garage was planned for Harold Price. However, it was not built as a garage but as a shop from where Price traded in hardware, coal, building materials and a yard and a bit of a garage behind where he parked his taxis. Chandon's proposal was approved by William Cowley, Chairman of the Newhaven District

Council in February 1923 but was never built in that form, only the hardware shop with its part-circular front shown in all of the photographs of Harold's store was built. The final development was rather a muddle of little buildings built at different times with Thrower and Woolgar's separate butcher's shop at the east end on plot 12, Harold Price's hardware shop, a half-finished cycle and electrical shop; somewhere there was a teashop and Mr Ferguson's second-hand furniture shop. Mr Larcombe's grocery store was built with its western boundary alongside Vernon Avenue. All of the little shops may be seen in photographs in this book. Perhaps Chandon's disappearance in France was the reason as to why the original development failed to go ahead. See figure 3.

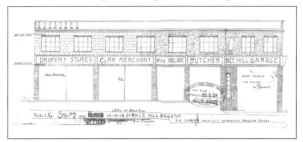

Vernon Chandon's Shop and Office development on Warren Road in 1923. Fig. 3.

In 1924 the Foulger brothers of Islingword Road, Brighton applied to the Newhaven Rural District Council to build a single two-bedroom bungalow with a kitchen, living room and an earth closet in the garden. Although the kitchen sink was shown connected to a cesspool the closet was not. The building was sited north of where Channel View Road was subsequently laid and the address given was Near Warren Road, Rottingdean. Mr Foulger became well known in the village and was to open a large ironmongers, and painter's and decorator's shop some years later.

Meanwhile, Harold Price had built himself a garage near to the bottom of Balsdean Road but could quickly see that the site was wrongly positioned because he missed out on passing traffic on the Downs Road, besides which I remember it being rather small for a garage. In June 1927 Harold applied for Planning permission to build a new garage a hundred yards below the cross-roads which was approved rather rapidly on the last day of that month. See photograph No 32 in THMP.

At this time there were a variety of buildings being put up for families from all walks of life, some were shacks typical of an early 20th century plot land development, a few railway carriages appeared, bought from the Lancing Carriage Works and often used only as holiday homes, some bungalows had asbestos-lined timber walls and asbestos slates and no foundations, but some were special and during the 1930s there were a few on the Wick and Downs Estates that would have graced any village in England. A number of very fine houses were built along the Falmer Road but what was striking were the lovely large gardens that can still be seen today. Unfortunately, many houses have been demolished in recent years and whereas the original building density had been only five houses per acre recent redevelopments have been carried out at the rate of twelve per acre and, as a consequence, the housing stock and the appearance of some areas of the village has suffered. I believe that some commentators in describing the village have been very unfair and wrong to compare it with other places such as Camber Sands and Bracklesham and the seaside development of Normans Bay. Whereas a number of surrounding villages have been swamped by suburban expansion our village has retained its original shape and size and is able, quite rightfully, to boast of the best sea views along the Sussex coastline. If you are unable to actually see the sea one can usually see the Downs. How many homes have a sea view in Rottingdean?

Life in "The Beehive"

This is the tale of a family who have lived in Woodingdean for many years some of which was spent in a beehive, well not actually a beehive, but a bungalow called 'The Beehive' in Crescent Drive. It is the story of the Cuthbertson family, a family with a very familiar name in the village for it was Duncan and Bessie Cuthbertson who came to the village in 1925 with their three children, William known as 'Jack', McClennan known as 'Douglas', and Mabel known as 'Babs', Richard, the youngest and always known as Dick, arrived during the following year and has lived in the village for eighty-three years except for three years in Norfolk and for a short while in Antarctica. It is fair to say that there are precious few families in the village whose past is so intrinsically linked with the history of the village from the earliest time. William was born in 1915, McClennon in 1919, Mabel in 1924 and Dick in 1926.

The family were drawn to Woodingdean from the Shires, an altogether different area of the country where the fields were small and bounded by woodland and coppices. Here on the open Downs the first sight revealed no such friendly vistas. William recalls seeing a long narrow black cinder path running straight down the slope of bare hillside to distant valleys and the far horizon of the sea. This was called The Ridgway with Darjeeling chicken farm at the top and another chicken farm owned by the Fairley's further down. Opposite was the Hardiment's large family house called 'Ridgway House' which appears in many of the early photographs of The Ridgway. The Hardiment family were immigrants from the diamond fields of South Africa and ran a dairy from an old bungalow at the bottom of the road. Opposite Fairley's was the new residence which Duncan and Bessie had high hopes of buying but turned out to be a dreadful disappointment. So disappointed were they with the asbestos 'shed' with its bare earthen floor they refused to move into the place and whilst Duncan went off to find some alternative accommodation Bessie stayed on the roadside with the children laying out blankets for the night! Fortunately the weather was very mild at the time and Mrs Fahey, a neighbour, seeing their plight suggested they all stayed in her house until morning. She also knew the unscrupulous man who had tried to sell them the shed as a house and was delighted to help the family to avoid his clutches. Mr and Mrs Fahey had two children who were to become good friends with the Cuthbertsons; Pat, their son, knew everything about motorbikes and daughter Myrtle gave up her bed for William who, to his dying day, could remember the romantic perfume of her pillow!

Meanwhile, Duncan had found an old barn at the top of Seaview Road and with plenty of straw to sleep on and a manger for little Mabel to sleep in they settled down. This was a happy time and the family stayed there for some time. The barn was situated on the Wick, and William could see for himself the dwellings around the farm, some were constructed in asbestos and corrugated iron or matchboarding, some were smartly painted but most were flimsy products of inexperienced hands and limited cash. There were old railway carriages, a stranded boat, army surplus huts and even a bell tent adapted to provide semi-permanent shelter while the occupants saved or strove to build or acquire more enduring homes. Often violent storms would sweep the structures from their foundations and scatter their contents far and wide. Repairing roofs with 'Ritto' was a common sight after a storm.

Duncan Cuthbertson was a photographer and journalist and had a small war service disability pension which provided enough income to buy a bungalow with an acre of garden in Crescent Drive for £400 from Charles Wade. The bungalow stood on plot number 356 and had wonderful views across the valley to Rottingdean and because he kept bees they promptly named the property 'The Beehive', one of the most iconic bungalows in Woodingdean. At the time Mr Ferguson acted as an "Estate Agent" from his small office on the Race Hill, as it was known, and it was through him that they purchased the bungalow. The walls of the bungalow were clad with matchboarding taken from the old dismantled army huts on Norton Top after the end of the Great War; nothing was wasted in Woodingdean at that time! However, the house was very cold and often they would find their chamber pots frozen over in the mornings, but it was a larger house than they had been used to in the Shires with two south-facing front rooms with French windows opening out onto a veranda. One front room served as a sitting room because it had the only fireplace, two of the others and a lean-to served as bedrooms, and the remaining large room at the rear was the kitchen/ living room complete with a 'Rippingill' paraffin cooking stove on which Bessie prepared a wide variety of delicious meals. There were no drains, sewers or gas, no water or electricity; the only light coming from oil lamps. There was no piped water supply for a long time apart from a tap at the top of Warren Hill and another opposite the Downs Hotel from where water could be delivered by donkey and cart for a penny a bucket in times of drought. Water was collected from the roof of the house and filtered through gravel beds and stored in a 6ft concrete water tank before being hand-pumped into a small tank in the loft. The toilet was situated in a small shed twenty feet from the house and consisted of a seat over the bucket and a nail for the bundle of newspaper or old catalogues for toilet use or reading matter. The bucket was emptied weekly to fertilize the vegetable plot where Bessie grew potatoes, vegetables, soft fruit and fine Cherry Rhubarb. Duncan kept bees, chickens and goats as most people did. One day a young lad was caught trying to take some honey from a hive so father gave him a bowl full saying 'you can eat as much as you can'; he was J Magee, who said he has never eaten honey since.

For entertainment they listened to a wireless powered by an accumulator that was recharged in Mr Stowell's small shop next door to Mr Goodenough's Post Office where they bought paraffin. Every ten days this process was repeated and would give them a chance to pick up some of their groceries which were not available on Messrs Groomes 'Trojan' van that served the village until after

'The Beehive' home of Duncan and Bessie and their four children William, McClennan, Mabel and Richard or 'Dick'.

the end of the war. Mr Smith delivered milk around the village in a horse and cart. During the dry summer months the roads were passable but in winter often there would be as much as two inches of gooey chalk hanging on to their shoes. On moonless nights hurricane lamps were essential to avoid ruts and deep puddles in the unlit roads. Dick Cuthbertson remembers the summer weekends when they would collect winkles from the rocks at Rottingdean and enjoy the simple pleasures of searching for small sea creatures in the pools. 'After walking home we had a good evening meal of winkles', he says.

The Downs were a beautiful playground. In the spring the Norton Top dew-

pond came to life with toads, newts, tadpoles and small water creatures which they collected in jam jars to take home. Rabbits were so numerous that the turf was as smooth as a bowling green. Blackberries for home-made jam and wild mushrooms for breakfast were picked after the autumn rains. Life for the children was simple, safe, close to nature and above all else very enjoyable, a life that now belongs to a different age.

Dick and Mabel Cuthbertson tend the bees in their garden of 'The Beehive'. Dick married Peggy Latham and they continue to live on the original plot of 'The Beehive'.

William now takes up the story when describing 'our surroundings'.

'The Beehive' faced south from about halfway up the slope of the valley side. We could look over the valley to the sea. Below us the old lynchets then clearly marked the edges of the fields which had once been ploughed. They followed the contours of the land where the slopes changed. Just a hundred yards below our house there was a sharp lynchet about six feet high marking the beginning of the steeper grade on which 'The Beehive' stood. Farther down the Downs Valley Road the ground became level enough for a football or cricket pitch. Another lynchet of only three or four feet marked the transition from this flat area to more gently rising ground. Presumably the siting of these lynchets may have depended on the profitability of arable versus grazing land - more land would be ploughed in times of high corn prices. Above 'The Beehive' there was a less well defined lynchet near the Balsdean track at the place where the hill slope became more gentle as it approached the crest of the hill.

In the valley itself there was then no arable though crops of hay were taken. A couple of acres of weed-infested land were still fenced with a willow hedge. This area appeared to have been tilled and planted for vegetables two or three years previously. There was no evidence of past or present cultivation between the Balsdean track and the Crescent Drive. It showed all the signs of neglect - the scatter of clumps of gorse up to 20 or 50 yards wide indicated that there had been probably no management, even for sheep or stock pasture, for about ten years, i.e. since the outbreak of the World War in 1914.

The areas beyond the Balsdean way to the top of Bullock hill and by the site of the now deserted farm were fallow and unfenced but the weeds in the fields - sainfoin, tares, salad burnet, charlock, poppy and eyebright showed that crops had been grown within the past few years for fodder or green manure.

There was a scattering of dwellings on the Crescent Drive - to the west were the Hall family at 'Roedean', Miss Collinson lived in the bungalow opposite and next door to her there was a well-kept railway carriage occupied by an ex-game keeper. He was always shod in hobnailed boots and I greatly envied the leather buskins he invariably wore over his spindly legs. Then there was the home of the family who at first delivered goods by a horse and cart but had recently built a shed to house a model-T Ford to extend their carting business. Next, another family, the Pinks, in a weather-boarded wooden house called 'Chesham Bois'. The Parsons were a little way to the south of the Crescent Drive with a garden backing on to three or four acres of market garden, then the Richardsons in the cottage opposite ours. On the east going up the hill lived the Cummings, the Salisbury family, the Sussoms, the Majors, the Camplins, the Jones, Aspinalls and one or two others towards the west on the Balsdean road. The Downs Valley Road was a grass path branching from the Crescent Drive opposite 'The Beehive', it went past an old occupied railway carriage and a brick-built house at the top of the rise on the other side of the valley.

The Dubois family (all grown up) lived in two wooden bungalows next to 'The Beehive'. On the Balsdean road there was a large deserted wooden bungalow with a floor of chalk subsoil. All the earth had been cleared away and the chalk levelled and smoothed to make a hard surface that looked as if it was made of solid stone. The Hamilton family lived there but just as we arrived they went away, never to return. They left the doors and windows wide open, and the house empty, except for some dog biscuits on a shelf. Over the years this building sagged and bent, eventually to rot away - it seemed such a waste because it had been built well.

Up at the Wick, on the Warren Road there was a butcher's shop for all the usual cuts of meat including sausages, faggots, beef dripping and bones for the dog. There was also a shop for tobacco, newspapers and sweets. In those days there were very few packed items. There were expensive toffees such as the individually wrapped 'Blue Bird' at 1d each - highly desirable but well beyond our financial reach. Slater's Stores at the crossroads dealt in a similar range of items as well as some groceries. Slaters also ran a lending library, loans cost 1d per week but the choice did not compare with the range offered by Boots (the chemists) or the Municipal Library in Brighton. Most things were sold from large tins, bottles or sacks. The best value for pennies were boiled sweets - acid and pear drops were the favourite at 2d (1p) per quarter pound (100gms). There were also highly scented 'Angels Whispers' lenticular discs of hard, suckable pastel-coloured sugar fondant each bearing a brief romantic word or two. Then there was the slab toffee which came to the shop in flat tin trays from which it was taken by the shop assistant who broke it into pieces with the help of a pair of shears and a toffee hammer. The quantity was then weighed out and packed in a little paper bag or square of brown or blue wrapping paper. Aniseed balls often as much as a penny each - though expensive were deemed good value - they lasted a long time and changed colour from the original or yellow to a wide variety of interesting hues, green, blue, red, and orange as they dissolved in the mouth until in the evening nothing was left except a single aniseed to remind one of their name and origin. There were monkey nuts otherwise known as peanuts, tiger nuts (not so popular), large dried carob bean pods with sweet but fibrous husks and hard inedible seeds, dried liquorice root - sweet but not as attractive as the sticks or ribbons of black liquorice at 4 for a penny and the loose liquorice 'all sorts' which were more costly than acid drops. There were a few affordable pre-wrapped sweets such as the sherbets. These were small triangular packets containing a powder and a small boiled sugar lolly at the end of a stick. This could be licked and moistened so that when dipped in the sherbet it became coated with a lemon or pear drop scented powder which tasted of sugar and fizzed in the mouth. There were also packets of 'Cavendish Cut' made to look like tobacco and 5 sticks of candy, white with red tips, in a packet labelled 'Woodbines' for a penny, just like the real Woodbines which then cost 2d for 5. Fizzy lemonade and carbonated, coloured drinks (but no fruit juices) were available in glass bottles - often returnable for a penny when emptied. There were no ice creams in the shops until the 1930s when the first electric refrigerator was installed in the village. Ices could occasionally be bought from an itinerant ice cream man on the sea front but very rarely on the inland villages. Milk was delivered daily, in glass pint bottles with cardboard caps from a local dairy farm. The bottles were labelled with the name of the dairyman and were marked with a line to define the depth of the cream layer.

In the summer holidays the children made kites from brown paper and wooden slats, Dick made balsa wood and tissue paper gliders and aeroplanes to fly over the Downs, they built four-wheel carts but suffered cut knees and iodine dressings as a result. If it wasn't iodine it was a bicarbonate to sooth the blistered arms and legs on the beach, a favourite haunt during the hot weather. Armed with a packet of sandwiches and a sixpenny collapsible beaker from Woolworths William would spend all day exploring the beaches and rock pools quite unlike those previously encountered at Hunstanton on the shores of The Wash. One day he fell off the concrete slipway and being unable to swim was rescued by a gentleman dressed in plus fours but not knowing what to do next William offered his hand in gratitude whereupon the gentleman walked him to Lucy Ann's sweet shop in the High Street where he regained his dignity and dried off before walking home. What upset him most was the loss of his favourite beaker.

The years rolled by until the time came to leave to follow their own careers, William became an academic with a Doctorate in Biochemistry and moved to Harefield to join Glaxo where he carried out research, finally being honoured with an OBE for his work as a nutritionist. He retired and moved back to the south coast and settled in Rottingdean where he died in 2003. He was always fond of the village and wrote short articles on local history. Douglas left the village at the start of WW2 to join the Foreign Office and lived in many parts of the world. He served in the war and still treasures his mother's and sister's moving letters when on active service. The letters were sent from 'The Beehive' and his mother describes their lives during the blackouts and expresses her worry for his safety. *'I follow anxiously in the paper this terrible German invasion into NE France, Jack and I talk and wonder where you are in all that awful melee of aeroplanes, vehicles, refugees, guns and bombs'.* Douglas married Amanda who became The Reverend Amanda Cuthbertson of the Parish of St Marks, Wellingborough. Mabel became a District Nurse and stayed single all her life, sadly she died in the 1980s in Handcross where she lived. Dick was the only sibling to stay in the village more or less all his life running a small business as a motor engineer at the bottom of McWilliam Road. He tried his hand in Norfolk as an agricultural engineer but returned to the village after three years and married Peggy Latham in 1962. Peggy lived in Vernon Avenue with her parents Reg and Annie and four siblings, Anne, Reg (junior), Helen and Josephine; two other children Maxine and Antony came along later but never lived in Woodingdean. Before that the family had lived at Cambridge Farm, an isolated little cottage on the Downs midway between Woodingdean and Falmer, but in 1937 they moved into a farmhouse high up on Newmarket Hill (see painting by Douglas Holland on page 34) until the military occupation in 1942 which necessitated them moving away and into Vernon Avenue where as a youngster I first met the family during the war.

Dick attended the Woodingdean Temporary Council School in the Church Hall in Downsway and eventually the Brighton and Hove Grammar School. Peggy went to the Warren Farm School, the new Woodingdean Primary School in what was the meadow and finally to Queens Park School.

One day Dick met up with a colleague who had been to Antarctica with the British Antarctic Survey and soon he was telling Dick of the wonderful sights he had seen and when an opening came along for Dick to go with him off he went for eighteen months as a diesel engineer at Halley Bay. Duncan Cuthbertson had been a very keen photographer and Dick inherited the same interest taking hundreds of photographs of the ice shapes and wildlife on the ice cap.

During the 1950s Dick, Ray Barton and Dick Salisbury created 'The Woodingdean Stock Car Team' and took part in stock car racing at Arlington, Westham, and Lydon Hill; Ernie Brazier, one of the village builders, was their keenest supporter. I remember well the old cars and trailers used to transport their vehicles from one race meeting to another; they were a common sight in the village. Eventually Dick tired of the motor trade and went to work at Ricardo Engineers in Shoreham on engine development staying there until his retirement in 1987. He was awarded the prestigious Society of Automotive Engineers, Arch T.

Lynda Wymark and Dick and Peggy Cuthbertson in 2009 in the garden of where 'The Beehive' once stood. Between them they have lived in the village for over 200 years! Lynda's family have lived in the village since the 1930s when her grandparents Amy and Alfie Elford started a smallholding and a pig farm. Her mother and father Bill and Bunny Ruffle were well known in the village and could often be found in the Happy Corner Café with the Newbury family with whom they were great friends. Bunny was also a great friend of my mother and on occasions would come along to the Downs Cricket Club matches. When Lynda left school her first thoughts were to work in the village and secure a position at the Post Office in Falmer Road which is where she met her future husband Jack who was working in the garage nearby. They were married in the Church of the Holy Cross in 1970 where later she served as a Churchwarden for seven years. She is still a keen churchgoer, sings in the church choir and helps out on all occasions particularly when decorating the church with flowers. Jack and Lynda had three children, Alan, Brian and Elaine while living in Brighton for a short time and eight grandchildren. They have lived in Balsdean Road for the last thirty years and their hobbies include gardening and caravanning. Jack helps out on the Vintage London to Brighton Car Run by towing the old crocks up Clayton Hill in his four-wheel vehicle.

Colwell Merit Award for his work on emission control which at the time was a relatively new science.

When they married, Dick and Peggy were gifted part of the land on which 'The Beehive' stood and they are still there in their bungalow surrounded by over one hundred different species of trees and shrubs that Dick has collected throughout the years. Dick enjoys wood carving and collecting ancient flint artefacts off the fields and in all his eighty-three years in the village has only moved a few yards and is not likely to move again. David their son attended the University of Aberdeen achieving a degree in Biophysics and their daughter Susan is with the Nuffield Hospital in Woodingdean as a Biomedical Scientist and, like their parents, lives in or near the village where they grew up.

The boy who walked and walked

Many years ago I remember walking home from Falmer Station to Woodingdean after an inter-school rugby match at Lewes and it was snowing hard, very hard, and my only protection against the elements was a school blazer. As I approached the top of the road out of Falmer village I was confronted with the decision of whether to continue on the road or take a more direct but shorter route across the snow-covered fields. I remember being very tired after the exertion of rugby but the snow was falling so heavily I decided to take the shorter route but looking southwards across the valley towards the village I could barely make out the houses along the Drove Road. My path would take me close to a small cottage on the hillside called Cambridge Farm, the home of an irascible elderly man known as Jack Nicholls who lived there with his nephew John who I always thought was also called Nicholls, but I was wrong, his surname was Munro but this did not come to light until just a few years ago. As I passed down the side of the bungalow Jack was chopping wood or engaged in some winter task which I cannot now recollect. The year I think was 1953. Jack stared at me in amazement as he hardly ever saw visitors and dropped what he was doing perhaps wondering whether I was up to no good. His gaze followed me for a while and when at last I did turn round I could see that he was chopping wood again.

Jack was a common figure in the village often seen at Mrs Newbury's 'Happy Corner Café' on the cross-roads sitting with a cup of tea so strong as to be almost undrinkable. Born in 1881 he served in the Great War and was gassed in the trenches which left him with

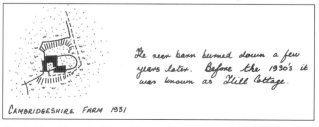

Cambridge Farm in 1931 after a name change from Hill Cottage, the home of Jack and May Nicholls and John Munro.

running eyes for the rest of his life. He was always happy to talk to people but would tease a plug of tobacco out of anyone that sat near him, hence his nickname 'Tobacco Jack'. He was often accompanied by a knobbly stick and wasn't shy of using it against cheeky kids. He dressed in a jacket, shirt but never a tie, leather gaiters, heavy boots and wore a pork pie hat, at least that is the image I have carried with me over the years. He was friendly and for several years my parents occasionally employed him to do the heavy digging in our garden. Jack was habitually crafty, constantly dropping hints that it was thirsty work, and I remember my mother saying that he spent more time drinking than gardening. He was, however, very strong and my parents recognized that he could dig better than anyone else and were happy to pay him the going rate of one shilling an hour or in today's money 5p/hr. After a while I got to know and like him and he would tell me all sorts of stories that he would make up on the spur of the moment. When I left the village I saw him no more. I do know that he had been a good boxer in his day and, although I never saw it, a picture of him in boxing attire hung on the wall in his cottage. He was very proud of that picture and from memory I was once told that he had been a champion boxer in the army. Certainly his face was a testament to his chosen sport. He was keen on football and followed the fortunes of the Woodingdean Football Club actually sponsoring the team after he won a few pounds on the football pools. On one occasion he got himself into trouble with a referee who he thought had made an unfair decision against 'his' team.

In their isolated location on the Downs, Jack's cottage was the only dwelling in one of the polling areas of the Parish of Falmer and Jack was the only voter. Jack became famous overnight and the Argus ran the story.

It was not until 2007 that I made contact with his nephew John Munro after he wrote to the Argus on the subject of the hamlet of Balsdean. This was followed up with a meeting with a group of old 'Woodingdeaners' all of whom remembered John and were keen to join us on a history walk to Balsdean. The appearance of John surprised me for I remember him as a tall young man always on a big old black bike that he bought for twelve shillings and sixpence (62$\frac{1}{2}$p in today's money) which he rode vigorously around the village but hardly any further, for John, like a number of villagers rarely left Woodingdean.

Hardship is a relative term and can mean many things to many people, whether it be caused by

'The boy that walked and walked', John Munro, in 1946, who lived at Norton Farm and Cambridge Farm midway between Woodingdean and Falmer. Only a scar on the downland turf now tells us of its precise location.

John Munro's uncle and aunt Jack and May Nicholls in the 1960s who also lived at Norton Farm and Cambridge Farm. Jack was known as 'Tobacco Jack' on account of his being able to tease a plug of tobacco from the innocent bystander. Jack was a good boxer in his day.

suffering, toil, fatigue, or the injustice of poverty, most of those terms applied to John who had more than his fair share of hardship as a boy, more so probably than any other person in Woodingdean. Life can be inherently unfair. In my teens he disappeared into hospital only to emerge a short while after as a very clean shaven young man. I have sat with John, a quiet man by nature, for a long time and this is his story.

He was born in Brighton in 1933 to parents Joseph and Kate Munro but lost his father, a door-to-door salesman when two years old and then tragically lost his mother three years later. As an orphan who never knew his parents he was taken in by his uncle and aunt Jack and May Nicholls to live with them in a very old leaky galvanised iron shack in Downland Road, Woodingdean where he remained until the outbreak of the war. Jack worked as a carter or horseman for Fred Hylden who was a slaughterman who also lived in Downland Road. Jack was also a farm labourer and in 1939 was offered a job by Guy Woodman who lived in the manor house at Balsdean Farm with their son Gerald. As part of the deal they were allowed to stay in Norton Farm Cottage which had no running water, electricity, gas or anything else which meant that John at the age of six had to walk alone every day in all weathers, come rain or shine and very often in the dark to Warren Farm School, a very long way for such a small lad. The family was very poor but often John was required to walk into the village for the groceries at Robinson's Stores and on one occasion, being very hungry, he bought a dozen penny buns which he finished off on his walk home. Being so young John is unable to recall too much now about Balsdean but he does remember that Norton Farm Cottage was a very cold house to live in. He does, however, recollect one particular Christmas Day, not because of any presents, but simply the 'bright and frosty morning'. In 1942 the Army arrived in the valley with tanks and Bren-gun carriers which signalled the start of the permanent evacuation of the hamlet. For a while the family stayed on but soon the valley was too dangerous for civilians and they were forced to leave. John remembers the soldiers and the equipment they brought into Balsdean and particularly recollects one soldier who, after spending a night in the Downs Hotel, tore his trousers on the barbed wire surrounding the hamlet and his aunt offering to mend them. It is an historical fact that John is now one of the very few living persons to have lived in the deserted village of Balsdean.

By now Jack was out of work but Harold West was looking for additional hands as part of his war effort to grow more corn for the nation. Wages were for the best part very low and farm labourers were expected to work long hours for little pay. Harold West allowed them to have Cambridge Farm, a small deserted cottage with a barn high out on the hill behind West's farm between Woodingdean and Falmer, the exact spot now barely discernible in the grass. The farm cottage had recently been vacated by Reg and Annie Latham who had lived there between 1935 and 1937 with their two young children, Ann and Reg.

Whilst Cambridge Farm was closer to civilisation it had no running water until many years later when a piped supply was connected to the farm, no gas or electricity, and for heating they depended on dried cabbage stalks, gorse and very occasionally a little coal was carried by hand with the lamp glasses and paraffin from Price's Stores in the village. Fourteen pounds in weight is all they could carry over the fields and that lasted for one night. Water was taken from a well but only when rainfall was sufficient. The postman called occasionally when the weather allowed, if not they collected what mail they had at the post office in Falmer.

The little flint-built cement-rendered cottage which was called Hill Cottage in 1899 had two rooms downstairs with plain matchboarded and plastered walls. Uncle, aunt and John used one of the rooms as a bedroom lying on bran pokes or sacks on the brick floor with an old coat and a blanket laid over him to keep him warm and his aunt and uncle alongside. There were no such luxuries as sheets but John was warm and that was the main thing. Their other room had a bare concrete floor and a copper to which a tap was added later but was never used, Aunt May preferring the two troughs outside in the yard for all their washing. Cooking was done on a range fuelled also by cabbage stalks and gorse. Often Jack would chop up firewood on the brick floor. The two first floor rooms were not used other than for storage. An outside toilet consisting of a bucket and seat served the family well! John remembers the cottage was always very cold, the winter of 1947 being the worst in living memory when he searched for clean ice to melt for a cup of tea. On one occasion a complaint was made about the condition of the cottage and Jack was forced to whitewash the whole of the interior. John had no social life whatsoever and didn't go to the village dances that we all went to. Girl friends were non-existent as there was no real proper home to take them back to, besides which no young lady would ever attempt to walk the distance day or night. His lack of social skills became apparent when he finally left the village to work at Papworth Everard but that was much later. After moving to Cambridge Farm in 1942 John attended the village school in Falmer but the daily walks continued, perhaps not quite so far and by this time he was a stronger nine-year-old. Sometimes when he got home he was sent off to the shops in Woodingdean and that was even further to walk! He went every day to school except when the weather was extremely inclement. He had a very happy time at school and enjoyed being taught by Miss Pasco and Miss Francis.

During the war the cottage was protected by blackout blinds but the window frames were so rotten there were few places to fix them. Foxes and owls were his constant companions during the day and night. In 1945 John was sent to the Lewes County Modern School and travelled by bus and later by train which meant more walking. He finally left school in 1948 to start work on Harold West's farm in January 1949 and continued to live at Cambridge Farm until 1955. His first farm job was on the threshing drum which he found to be unpleasantly cold but in the Spring he graduated on to tractors, in particular a Case Dex fitted with a furrow press, but the tractor was prone to stalling which necessitated him having to walk a mile to get help to restart the engine as he was still too small to start it by himself. Life became more pleasant as time went by and soon John became a valuable worker gaining the skills needed at the time.

Two years after starting work his aunt died leaving John and Jack to fend for themselves in particularly difficult and sad times. Her coffin was carried shoulder-high from the cottage across the fields to the hearse waiting on the nearby track leading to Bevendean, a scene that John would never forget for it was May who had raised and cared for him from a very young age. He had nothing as a lad and fought for everything he had but to this day he has no regrets and remembers his aunt and uncle only with affection. Unfortunately, Jack's health deteriorated and in 1958 he was taken to live in a home in mid-Sussex where he remained for a time before going on to Worthing where he died peacefully, aged 89, in 1970.

Conscription into the services was an issue all boys faced in the 1950s but when John reported for his medical an X-Ray revealed a shadow and he was sent to hospital in Lewes for treatment for three months. Perhaps it was his exposure to the elements for all those years that had taken its toll. In March of that year John left hospital and went to see Harold West who was very pleased to see him and ushered him into the office where Peggy West greeted him with £25 back wages, a lot of money in those days, particularly for John. An act of kindness he was never to forget.

In 1955, at the age of twenty-two, John embarked on a new career and joined Papworth Everard as trainee vehicle body-builder at fifty shillings a week and it was there he met and married Rosemary in 1967. He was to stay for forty-six years. Along the way John and Rosemary produced two sons, James and Michael both of whom kept well away from farming.

John says 'with all the ups and downs I still remember this as happy times and shall carry these memories for the rest of my life. I didn't have a good start in life but did well in the end'.

He still occasionally comes back to Woodingdean and pays his tribute to the West family who many years ago gave him shelter and the support he needed.

See page 75 of THMP for further information and a plan of Cambridge Farm.

Ivor and the Doodlebug

Ivor Levett was a village lad who grew up during the 1930s and the war years and like all the older boys in the village at the time was interested in how we were repelling Hitler's armies and how they could do their bit for King and Country. With his pals Ivor would try and be first on the scene of anything that was interesting, or better still dangerous, including downed war planes and for collecting spent or even live bullets and fragments of stray bombs at Balsdean before anyone else could find them.

On one such occasion Ivor nearly went too far, this is his story.

On the 5th July 1944 at about 6:30pm, I, along with one of my Woodingdean friends, was out cycling along the Woodingdean to Falmer road in the vicinity of the old dew pond when the drone of a V1 Doodlebug was heard. We saw it approaching from the southeast and as it grew larger in the sky the engine spluttered and died. We, along with unseen nearby residents, waited in fear of where the explosion would occur. As it was not directly in our line we watched as it grew larger and as it was gradually losing height it was obvious that it was going down on a line slightly east of Falmer Village.

We waited with baited breath expecting an explosion as it dipped out of view. There was no explosion, so we, as two young adventurers, peddled fast and furious towards the landing area. We found it sited on the two front gardens of the cottages at the NW corner of Balmer Lane at the junction with Lewes Road, now commonly called the A27. As we rode around the rear of the V1 we stood with amazement that we were so near to the bomb never fearing that it might have had a delayed explosion. People were standing at the front of the two cottages and like us were not showing any signs of panic. This was World War II, where it took a lot to disturb the residents.

Probably a quarter of an hour elapsed while we gazed in awe at this dreaded German weapon, when up cycled a policeman puffing away on his push bike. After asking where we came from, he told us in no uncertain terms to return to Woodingdean or our names would be in his pocket book. Knowing that we would also incur the wrath of our parents, we made a tactical withdrawal.

Even to this day, if you stand slightly to the west of Balmer Lane junction and face south you will see that the trees on the far side of the modern dual carriageway have a section which is lower than the adjacent trees. This is because the V1 actually scythed through those trees leaving the permanent reminder for those who remember that incident. Not many people had the experience of standing that close to an unexploded V1. The only other damage as I recall was to the well-tended kitchen gardens of the cottages. In those days of food shortages this would have been a great loss to the families, cutting off their source of fresh produce.

Even after the ensuing years, the memories return each time I pass that spot.

The staff of the East Sussex Records Office inform me that of all the incidents of V1s recorded in East Sussex, there were only two on the west side of Lewes but hundreds to the east. There were no recorded press announcements as the policy in the war was not to give information out to the general public.

Ivor Levett was born in 1932 but sadly lost his mother Constance when only a few months old. His father Ernest, a Polegate man, came to Woodingdean where he got remarried to Annie Whyman known to all as 'Nance'. However, the early 1930s were uncertain times and whilst Ernest looked for work, young Ivor was sometimes looked after by friends including Wally and Doris Chapman in The Ridgway. Ivor started school at the Warren Farm School becoming friendly over the years with Sam Woolgar, John Martin, Graham and John Burchell, Terry Keller, Julie Pannett, Joyce Russell, Pat Butler, Margery Sweetman, Margaret Robinson, Colin West, Alan Healey, Sid Goodenough and Len Norris. He went on to the Brighton Intermediate School which had previously been bombed necessitating the school to be shared with the girls on an alternating morning /afternoon basis. He left there in 1948 to join GPO Telephones as an apprentice engineer where he stayed for forty-one years until retirement.

Ivor's father joined the navy as a boy entrant but was invalided out, eventually joining the GPO but, due to the depression of the late twenties, the last in were the first out and so he got a job with Mr Price at his shop in Warren Road and also in his garage where he served petrol. Ernest became a very well-known character in the village as he delivered materials to all Price's customers. During the war he moved employment to the Brighton Radio Circuit Ltd which provided piped programmes around the town. He stayed there until his retirement aged seventy.

During school holidays Ivor helped out on the farms with the Land Army girls always looking forward to the arrival of the traction engine with Mr Stepney at the wheel. On one occasion Ivor was helping a farm hand and a Land Army girl collecting sheaves with a tractor and trailer in a field to the east of the Woodingdean - Falmer road near the dew pond when a German fighter plane flew low up Bevendean Valley heading straight for them, being shot at by the men firing the Ack Ack gun at the top of Vernon Avenue. Swiftly poor Ivor was bundled under the trailer. There was a lot of gunfire as the plane approached and even after it had flown on over their heads the bullets were still whistling past. The first time the gunners would have seen the plane it must have been at their level as it came up through the valley until it disappeared from view over Newmarket Hill. Luckily the gunners were not good shots, if they had been it was likely that the plane may have hit Ivor and the others. At this time Ivor was living at the top of Vernon Avenue with his parents and would often go up and talk to the gun crews and sit on the gunner's seats and raise and lower the turret or the other seat that rotated the gun. Ivor's recollection is that the unit may have been bound for the 8th Army in El Alamein as the trucks and Quads with field guns and limbers were sand coloured. There was also a unit with Bren gun carriers and one weekend he was offered a ride, an offer he could not refuse. They went off down Vernon Avenue and his father was painting the bungalow when he looked up and saw him; his expression turned to stone. They went over the Race Hill down Manor Hill, an unmade road in those days into Whitehawk, along to Roedean, then up alongside the East Brighton Golf Course and back home. Father was not best pleased and Ivor's ears stung for a long time, but it was worth it. Ivor also remembers The Princess Patricia's Canadian Light Infantry billeted in the village - a mad lot who used to throw thunderflashes around to put the wind up the kids. They were present at the D-Day landings and fought their way through to Caen where a number died and are remembered in that city. Other Ack Ack guns were set up with searchlights in Sheepcote Valley and when the boys came out of Mrs Jenner's boys club around nine o'clock they would often go up to the bus shelter to watch the action, a pastime that again earned a clip round the ear from their dads. No health and safety in those days!

Many of the lads in the village took an active interest in the aircraft that came down on the hills around the village, sometimes they would race to the scene to beat the Home Guard or the policeman to get a souvenir or trophy. A barrage balloon landed in Happy Valley sometime during the war and was guarded by RAF personnel.

There were four British planes that came down; the first was a Spitfire on the 19th August 1940 during the Battle of Britain on Bevendean Farm when Pilot Sgt Johnson attached to 175 Forward Corp made a crash landing having run out of fuel. The crash was not reported to the police although the plane was slightly damaged. The pilot survived to walk through the village on his way back to his airfield. In 1941 a second plane, a Boston Havoc No BB890, on a practice flight from Ford crash-landed on the Falmer Road half a mile north of the Downs Hotel when both airscrews stopped. Pilot Sgt Lasche survived uninjured. The third was on the 24th April 1943 when a Mosquito crash-landed killing Sqn Ldr Bocock and Pilot Sgt Robert Brown from 605 Squadron, Ford. The reason for the crash was not established but both men were very badly burned. The last plane, a "Waco" Glider, fell at Loose Bottom, Falmer on the 3rd April 1945. The glider was being towed but was cast off from the towing Dakota due to "speed and turbulence of wind current". The two-man crew were uninjured.

The old church hall was used by the army and many a packet of chewing gum was passed to the boys from there. When the new church was built in 1941 Ivor joined the choir and became head choirboy. He left when he was about fifteen years old. He was a keen cyclist and with some of the village lads would cycle to far-away places as Hastings, Tunbridge Wells and even Portsmouth, which in the days of heavy old bikes was an extraordinary journey. To earn a little more money Ivor worked part-time in the village garage in the early 1960s and married Jacqueline or Jacie as she was affectionately known in February 1960. Jacie trained as a nurse and they first moved into Crescent Drive South then moved permanently to Billinghurst nine years later. They are blessed with three children Sandra, Lois and Darren who between them have produced six grandchildren.

Ivor loves to recount his childhood memories, particularly the years during the war and the period of austerity just after when life on the Downs could be very hard on some, but luckily Ivor could see the funny side of most things and is still able to recollect the more humorous occasions. As a schoolboy his journey took him to the top of Elm Grove where one day the No2 bus conductor jumped down from the bus to visit the Gents toilet which they often did, but on this occasion the passengers got on the bus rather quickly, and the last lad that got on pressed the bell and the driver drove off leaving his conductor in the toilet. Naturally this caused a great deal of laughter and it was not until they got to Warren Hill that the conductor caught up on the back of a motorbike.

The lady who made cream buns

When it became known that London children would be evacuated out of the city into the country, Doris and Herbert Keller, or Bert as he was called, decided otherwise and set off for Brighton in search of a small business from which they hoped to make a living. Doris and Bert had a greengrocer's shop in Morden where they lived and, with two sons Roy and Terry to look after, they were keen to make an honest living in running a shop.

They settled in Woodingdean in about 1939 where they bought a small baker's shop in Warren Road that was being run by two elderly women more or less as a hobby. At this time Roy was about eight years old and Terry was six. Mum and dad immediately placed both boys in nearby Warren Farm School which must have been quite a shock, but they survived and made plenty of friends. From there they eventually went on to Fawcett School.

Living opposite the working Warren Farm with its mid-19th century flint barns was very different to urban life in London and the boys soon enjoyed their new-found freedom on the Downs and in the fields and woods around the village. John Martin, Ivor Levett, Len Blackman, Ken Carney, Lennie Norris and Roy Pate soon were to form a ring of friendship around the boys, a friendship that has lasted to this day. Whilst Doris ran the shop selling bread and cakes delivered daily (most probably by the Stevens brothers) Bert, who was good at figures, having worked in an office in Covent Garden, found a job as a milkman in Brighton and the whole family was settled in and doing well. As the war progressed, Doris was able to get bread but fancy cakes were phased out, however, penny buns were still available so Doris bought some icing sugar which she made into a creamy mixture and put it into the buns. They were an instant success and Doris was sold out everyday.

As cake supplies dwindled Doris had the back wall of the shop altered to provide open access to the rear room where she set up tables and began serving teas with her helpers Jean Lazenby, Jean Tree and another girl called Ruby. Land Army girls from the farm opposite were good customers and if they were in the shop when they should have been working and the foreman came along they would throw themselves onto the floor until he was gone.

By this time the shop was known as the 'Thistle Cake Shop' rather than the colloquial name of 'Kellers'. Immediately next door lived a French lady Marie Saunders with her two sons John and Ron and daughter Marie. By now Doris was serving lunches as well as teas and when she was very busy she would bang on the kitchen wall and Marie would go round to help out. Marie helped out with Terry's french homework! but sadly by this time Doris and Bert were growing apart and their marriage ended in divorce. As D-Day approached the adjacent shop became vacant and a number of soldiers from a Canadian Regiment 'The Princess Pats' were billeted there. Doris' Café became their NAAFI and she opened it up to them in the evenings where they could have refreshments and food and write letters home.

In 1948 Terry left school and the two boys and Doris moved to a smallholding in Blackboys near Uckfield where they remained until 1955. In later years the boys had left home and Doris remarried. Roy and Terry both tried their hands working for a local builder but were eventually to go into the Royal Air Force for their national service after which Roy joined the Surrey Constabulary and Terry the Eastbourne Constabulary, both serving the full thirty years of service.

Doris was an accomplished pianist having spent time playing at a London cinema during the days of silent films. She also played the piano on special occasions in the foyer of the Church of the Holy Cross. After remarrying Doris went on to run a Youth Hostel near Dorking, eventually settling in a bungalow near Guildford where she died aged eighty-two in 1990. Her husband Bert returned to Woodingdean after a short spell in London and died there in 1996.

A group of old timers in the Downs Hotel sometime during the 1930s. Whilst most of the faces are recognisable their names have been lost in time.

I have good reason to remember the cake shop as on many occasions as a young lad I pressed my face against the window and secretly yearned for just one small cake or a halfpenny bread roll. On one memorable occasion during the winter of 1947 I remember my mother giving me four and a half pence (old pence!) for a large loaf. After I collected it from the shop I ate a lump out of the end as I wandered slowly up the twitten into Farm Hill. The snow was a foot deep and as I tried to open the back door I dropped the loaf down the drain. I don't recollect what happened next...

Constable Jack Walton standing proudly outside Police Box No 27 in the 1950s. Jack was very popular and helped many people in the village over the years. The Police Box stood outside the Downs Hotel and was there for over thirty years.

The Woodingdean Football Club in 1929-30. Councillor Weymouth was President and Mr Pavey Vice President. Shown also are Mr Pavey's two sons, Wally Chapman, Ernie Souch, the Harman brothers and several other village lads.

The football team in the late 1930s taken at their wooden changing hut at the top of Falmer Road.

Back row L to R - Cyril Tasker, Harry Dynan, and ? Ross. Centre - Fred Johnson, Robin Goodenough and Ray Robinson. Front - Geoff Parsons, Harry Wellar, ? Randal, Brian Mason (mascot), Albert Johnson and John Saunders.

An extract of the Rules of the Woodingdean Football Club in 1938 - when players were fined sixpence for using abusive or obscene language - as if footballers would!

The Grocer's Shop in Rudyard Road in 1952 with proprietor George Stevens, assistants Frances and Elizabeth Stevens and a young Yvonne Mitchell. A young customer slips in behind to find the sweet jar. Chocolate and sweets had only been off ration for less than a year when the picture was taken.

Alfie Dove on the right, a well-known character in the village, celebrates in the Downs Hotel with Wally Todd having won through the qualifying rounds and reached the major Competition of the News of the World Individual Darts Championship of London and the South of England in 1939. Alfie was a founder member of the Downs Hotel Darts Club, a village club that was keenly supported and known in the area as being a very formidable outfit. Alfie came from Brighton with his young wife Violet in the late 1920s and at first lived in a humble little bungalow on Crescent Drive that was as much tin as brick, but he, like them all at that time, worked hard and soon took a rented bungalow in

Vernon Avenue where their six children Peggy, Gladys, Dorothy, Derek, Irene and Reg grew up. Alfie had a variety of jobs and Violet worked with Peggy at the Warren Farm School. Derek started work at the age of 14 at Alan West and met a young Thelma Colwell who came to the village in 1952. They courted and married in 1960 at the Holy Cross Church. They still live in Woodingdean and have two sons, Gary and Alan.

The village 'Rounders Team' 1929. The location is unknown and the faces sadly forgotten.

The Warren Farm Industrial School and the Well

The story of the School is told in THMP and WR&TM.

The population of Brighton exploded between 1801 and 1851 from 7,339 souls to 65,569 and by 1879 it stood at approximately 99,522. Brighton was one of two towns that had 'benefited' from a net immigration of people from London and from the rural economy that lay in tatters throughout Sussex. The proletariat labourer devoid of his 'customs in kind' way of life entered the town with his ragged family to seek work that was near impossible to find. Many were vagrants and tramps and these in particular were not encouraged to stay. The overcrowded workhouse in the centre of the town was so full that in 1820 the Guardians purchased a nine-acre site on Church Hill off what was to become Dyke Road and an Architect by the name of George Mackie was appointed to build a new workhouse with John Cheeseman a local builder.

Ten thousand pounds was granted for the project and the Bishop of Chichester, the Reverend D Carr, was invited to lay the foundation stone carved from a piece of stone dug up on the site. The frontage was 191 feet and the building was shaped as an 'H' with separate quarters for the sexes, and inmates were classified from adult down to children aged six. It was a frightful place where 'soup leftovers' were regularly served as a way of offsetting the high cost of bread and beer served to adults twice a day, one pint at dinner and another at supper to supplement the cheese. Children were given two half pints in a similar fashion. Why the beer, because the water in the town was contaminated by local cesspits.

The Church Hill Workhouse eventually had many problems; boys and girls were troublesome, rude and very abusive to those in contact with them. Many had simply been abandoned by their parents as they moved on to find local lodgings or to find work in other towns. Offending children were treated harshly for their sins being given hard labour as the favoured punishment or sentenced to the House of Correction. Often children slept four or five in a bed and became uncontrollable, and as a way of getting them off the parish and easing the burden on the Poor Law Ratepayers the Guardians ordered a number to be transported to Australia. That, however, was later discouraged. At this time Brighton was flooded out with new public houses and alehouses, one observer saying that there was one pub to thirty houses in the centre of the town. Alcohol fuelled crime, burglary was rife, interpersonal crime widespread and the more sophisticated crimes from London eventually got a hold. Brighton was unique and crime was also.

A report in 1847 concluded that 'the lack of separation exposed the workhouse children to bad examples from persons of mature age who were likely to exercise influence over their minds'. Seven years later in 1854 the Poor Law Board gave permission for Brighton to purchase land for a new workhouse and a separate industrial school for the children in what was then in the parish of Rottingdean. The children were about to be saved from pauperism. In 1858 land for the new "Warren Farm Road" from Elm Grove to the new site was purchased from William Mabbott of Falmer and a year later Mr Edward Sattin was appointed Workhouse Master at Church Hill and his wife appointed Matron.

Construction of the new Warren Farm Industrial School finished in 1860 and in 1862 seventy-seven boys and sixty-six girls marched happily with their own band through the town and over the downs to their new home. Five years later all the adult inmates at Church Hill were transferred to the new Workhouse at the top of Elm Grove and the old workhouse was sold. Between 1859 and 1864 over 20,000 paupers had been admitted to the Church Hill workhouse.

The main school buildings of the Industrial School were completed in 1860 by the builders John Fabian of Brighton who had recently completed Brighton Station. In other words he was a fairly large builder although he also carried out small building works, for instance in 1855 and 1856 he provided estimates for a new pulpit and new door to St Margaret's Church, Rottingdean.

The form of tender for the construction of the Warren Farm Industrial School is not known but we must assume that Fabian's won the contract in competition; George Maynard was appointed the Surveyor.

George Maynard had six children but it was his fourth child, Sarah Maynard who became best known as the wife of Magnus Volk who she married on the 28th September 1850 at the Parish Church of St Nicholas, their marriage being solemnised by the Reverend C. E. Douglas. They started married life together in high spirits at 35, Western Road, a fair sized house with a shop in a first-class position; and there, in October the following year their son Magnus (junior) was born. Thirty-four years later Magnus Volk opened the Volks Electric Railway on the seafront at Brighton and in 1892 opened The Rottingdean Railway or the 'Daddy Longlegs' as it came to be known.

George Maynard was born in Eastbourne in 1801 and started life as a carpenter becoming an architect and surveyor before moving to Brighton in 1839 or shortly thereafter where he bought property in the Western Road area. When he was about fifty years of age he was appointed 'Surveyor and Assessor for the Parish of Brighton' just in time for him to design the Warren Farm Industrial School in 1858.

He was a man of substance and since he was dealing with the public purse then almost certainly he would have ensured that Fabian's won the contract by competitive means. The contract sum was £8,223 excluding the cost of the barns and the boundary wall fronting Warren Road. The ten-acre site cost £2,000 and they were able to purchase more land as the school expanded.

Orphans from the old workhouse at Church Hill took up residence under Mr and Mrs Hales, the first superintendents of the school. Originally the school had only a small farm but its importance grew to provide more produce for home consumption and for other institutions in

Probably one of the earliest photographs of the Warren Farm Industrial School with the Infirmary in the foreground taken around the turn of the century. Only sections of the boundary wall remain.

the Newhaven Union. Other barns were added along Warren Road and the four workers' cottages in 1906. In 1875 they rented the field near the entrance of the Warren Plantation and in 1900 added a further thirty-one acres of rented ground. The success of the school demanded more land and a year later they purchased another six acres alongside the cinder track (Old Parish Lane) and the Wick Barn for £750. Mr Beard the landowner and farmer offered them the

Warren Farm School Band demonstrating their fine skills during the 1920s. Mr Wells, seen here, taught boys to become fine musicians who later entered Army service bands, particularly the West Kent Regiment, The 5th Dragoon Guards, The 9th Lancers and The Sussex Regiment. Sometimes a group joined the same regiment together for companionship.

The School band in 1923 at a music festival where they regularly took fist prize. It is believed that the photograph may have been taken in Preston Park.

whole of the north end of Wick farm for £1,800 and a further seventeen acres on the west side of the Ovingdean Road (now the Falmer Road) for twenty-five pounds an acre.

In 1858 a new road for carriages called "Warren Farm Road" was laid over the Race Hill from Elm Grove to the School at a cost of cost £5,269 and was maintained jointly with Steyning Beard who needed access across it but, as he

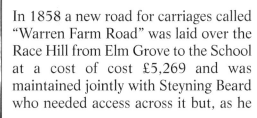

The Lodge situated at the west entrance of the driveway in the 1930s. It was demolished in the 1960s for road widening.

Douglas Holland's iconic painting of Warren Farm and the School.

was broke much of the time through gambling could ill afford to do so. In 1908 just before Beard died with substantial debts he agreed to rid himself of the expense of maintenance which then enabled the Guardians to make up the road with stone as a precondition to final adoption by the ruling Newhaven Rural District Council as a public highway.

The School from the west in the 1930s.

Many of the orphans admitted to the school came from the poorer parts of Brighton and London, some were deserted by their parents but no matter where their homes were all received a tolerable education based on Christian principles. The school was built to accommodate 360 children but by the turn of the century the number had dropped to 300 and by 1907 only 241, but by the start of the Great War it had increased again to 270. In 1909 one hundred and

Warren Farm School children take their midday rest in the meadow alongside the cinder track or Old Parish Lane as it now is. The Church Hall completed in 1928 is to the right. Notice how narrow Downsview Avenue was when it was part of the original road between Ovingdean and Woodingdean. The cinder track, as it was always known, dates back to the Saxon period and legend has it that King Charles II walked along it on his escape to France.

forty-eight children were discharged. Numbers swelled when troop movements to France increased in the Folkestone area as families were displaced in the town. Sudden increases put a burden on the Brighton Sanatorium where children were admitted when ill and as late as 1918 many were still being admitted from Folkestone and London. By 1920 circumstances for admission had changed, many children and babies who were baptised at the school were admitted by reason of their mothers being chargeable and by 1933 the school was opened to village children for primary and junior education following the closure of the Temporary Council School in Downsway. Mr Peach was appointed the first headmaster and under his leadership things improved and the children enjoyed a happier atmosphere.

In September 1939 a day before the start of WWII many of the children were evacuated to Brighton as it was felt that the School buildings should be made available as an auxiliary hospital. The period of notice to quit was no more than 24 hours but in that time the girls were taken to 24 and 25 Sillwood Road and the boys to 5 and 8 Portland Place; fourteen small children remained in one of the cottages at the School and fifteen, an unusually high number of children, also remained in the School hospital. Mr Horace Webb, Public Assistance Officer at the time, stated in March 1940 that *'a breaking up like this naturally curtails some things, such as outdoor sports in the way of football and netball. Nevertheless, with the approach of the better weather the close proximity of both places to the sea will enable the children to make full use of the beach, an amenity that was not so readily available to them in their old home. Many of the children can swim, and some of the boys attend swimming classes every week'.* Mr Webb went on to say that he could clearly see the definite advantages of being brought into closer active contact with town life and organizations which enable them to mix more freely with other children, and a more normal home life are definite advantages. He said *'it is true that in the private houses they are of necessity living under more limited and more confined conditions than they experienced at Warren Farm, but at the same time there is a more normal homely atmosphere. Naturally, the general administration and the catering and so on are somewhat more difficult, but the Homes Sub-Committee, the Superintendent and the Matron Mr and Mrs Ferriman and their staff are enthusiasts in their work. It can fairly be said that from the point of view of the happiness of the children the advantages out- weigh the objections'.* The significance of this last observation lies in the fact just prior to the war a final decision was about to be reached with regard to the establishment of a group system of village homes.

The two houses in Sillwood Road had approved accommodation for 36 children but the actual number in residence was only 31. Similarly the approved accommodation occupied by the boys was 78 and the actual number in residence was 57. The girls had the added advantage of a radio, a facility that was shortly to be provided for the boys. All the children appeared to be happy helping with the domestic chores and the girls were shortly to start knitting for the Forces when the wool arrived. A point of criticism was made about overcrowding in the dormitories and since the Warren Farm School had been used for purposes other than that of a hospital it was asked why the children could not move back. The Ministry of Health, however, still required the School to be immediately available as an auxiliary hospital and that if the children were to return then they may have to be moved again at a moment's notice.

The girls loved being in Brighton, albeit the war was now on, and for being able to shop and mix with the crowds in the town. The boys missed their football, however, and preferred the open spaces of the School. The evacuation was fairly short-lived and all the children were eventually moved back to the School.

Douglas Holland's interpretation of where the School's barns were situated in relation to the modern Woodingdean Library. They were beautiful barns where children played in the meadow alongside. In the lower picture the Schools swimming pool enclosure walls can just be seen between the pair of cottages and the gable-ended barn on the road.

Rear view of the School in 1994 prior to demolition, so ending 134 years of educating children.

By 1942 Woodingdean was declared an evacuable area because of its close proximity to the channel coast and it was expected that the evacuees would be happier away from the areas of greater danger. In March 1941 forty-eight boys and eighteen girls were evacuated to Edlington in Lincolnshire where they remained until Easter of the following year. With the reduction of staff at the School young children aged between three and five were transferred to the Schools Infirmary block at the rear of the School, the remainder aged up to sixteen being transferred to the four cottages Hazel, Oak, Ash and Beech Cottages. That was the last time the Infirmary was used at the School.

The School's farm workers were a very common sight in the village and in 1906 four cottages were built to house them, two on the cinder track and two on Warren Road. In 1903 Mr Arlett became Head Stockman and Mr King the ploughman and both were to live with their families in the cottages. The two cottages on Warren Road were demolished in 1947 to make way for the present Youth Hut. Mr King appears in a number of photographs with 'Prince' his favourite plough horse who was retired by the School aged 27 in 1941.

In 1946 the School finally closed its doors to orphans but was to remain open as a school. In 1955 the St John Baptist Roman Catholic Primary School became established there but changed its name to the Fitzherbert School which finally closed in 1987. After the terrible fire that destroyed the Wick Barn on the cinder track in 1947 the school farm was gradually closed down also. After the Fitzherbert School closed, the building lost much of its slate roof in the great storm of October 1987 and the building was vandalised.

Although a number of suggestions were put forward as to its continued use none were found to be viable and the site was eventually sold to the Nuffield Hospital in 1994 after which it was demolished. I was interested to look at the old well and had the pleasure of being there on the day that the concrete lid was removed to reveal its dark secrets and to measure the depth and level of the standing water which for the record was 385 feet below ground level, only 15 feet higher than the level in 1862. On that day and in front of television cameras I drank the water, most probably the first time that had been done for eighty years and have retained a jar of the water since for eventual analysis to ascertain whether the chemical composition changed from the samples taken in 1862 and recorded in THMP page 234.

In October 1995 history closed that chapter of our eventful past and heralded a new beginning with the coming of the Nuffield Hospital. Mrs Joyce McConnell recorded her thoughts in 'Monitor', the Newsletter of the Sussex Nuffield Hospital Spring 1994.

'While many technological advances have been achieved, the need for expansion has long been recognized and we can now look forward to being able to provide a number of additional services in our new hospital in Woodingdean.

It will enable us to treat a larger number of patients, offer a wider range of advanced facilities, health screening services and treatments, and to increase our links with local communities...'

The new Nuffield Hospital was opened by Her Royal Highness the Duchess of Kent and Mrs Joyce McConnell was appointed the first Hospital manager. My wife and I had the pleasure of being invited to the ceremony.

The Well

The famous well situated near the entrance to the Nuffield Hospital on Warren Road is the oldest structure in Woodingdean and when I peered down it in October 1994 the brickwork was as sound as the day when the steiner built it in a dark red and grey engineering brick. At the top the wall was 9 inches (225mm) wide. The Well provided the School with a very necessary independent supply of clean potable water that for centuries had been difficult to obtain in Brighton. Other sources of supply had been investigated for the School but were found to be unviable. A plan to pump water from the well over the Race Hill to the newly-opened workhouse at the top of Elm Grove was hatched, the main criteria being that the Guardians would be able to save money. However, with the well barely producing enough for the School the grand plan was finally shelved.

One source of supply for the town that was investigated and put forward in 1825 involved the construction of a clean water relief canal linking the river Ouse at Lewes with a new lake in Richmond Place, Brighton. The canal was to have run through Cranedean alongside the Lewes Road, pass under the Woodingdean - Falmer Road through a tunnel where the water was to run through a series of locks relying on gravitation for flow. The canal was to pass through the Bevendean Valley then alongside the old Lewes Road where the water would be finally collected and stored in the lake in the centre of the town.(ESRO QDP). Needless to say the project was rejected on the grounds of cost.

During the demolition of the School the nation's deepest hand-dug well was exposed to the world, the unique occasion being captured for posterity on television. The well has a measured depth of 1285 feet or 391.67metres and not only is it the deepest hand-dug well in Great Britain but possibly the world.

The well was started on the 25th March 1858 and completed when water was found on the 16th March 1862. A mural of my diagram, much copied by others, may be seen in the entrance to the Nuffield Hospital and the well can be viewed outside as a permanent historic feature. When I looked down the well for the very first time I was able to see some one hundred and fifty feet of the upper shaft and it was very noticeable that the brickwork was still in a sound condition without any cracks or buckling just as though it had recently been built. However, the walls of the lower shaft have been submerged for over 150 years and may tell a very different story. After flooding at the rate of 400 feet per hour all of the men's tools, lamps, windlasses and other gear at the four lower platforms were trapped in the shaft and remain there to this day. Initially the water rose very quickly but slowed to a height of 804 feet within 36 hours and remained at that height until it stabilised at 100 feet in the upper shaft. All told, the Guardians bought and paid for an estimated 238,000 bricks weighing about 530 tons.

Yield in the lower shaft was 50,000 gallons per day and in the upper shaft 1000 a day. Water temperature was reported as being 9.9C.

The lifespan of the School has passed into history and the new flagship hospital now stands on the site of where those poor men toiled unremittingly below ground, poorly paid, poorly fed, labouring tirelessly to be given only a simple medal and a dinner at the Town Hall. No other recognition was given them and although the story of the sinking of the well is recorded in THMP and other documents, including the Internet, other additional information has come to light during the intervening years, none more so than the names of those poor souls who dug it.

Samuel North, a well digger, was appointed by the Guardians in March 1858 to dig to the 400-foot level where they expected to find water, but none was found despite him digging down a further exploratory 38 feet in order to construct a heading. No water was found anywhere and after some delicate negotiations with North the Guardians decided to go it alone with their own supervisor and cheap labour force from the workhouse.

They took advice from Henry Catts, two local plumbers, Mr Bonner of Edward Street and Mr Smith of Ship Street and a Mr Heasman described as a 'practical man' of Upper Russell Street who all descended the well 'with an open mind' to investigate the problem and hopefully find water. None was found, only 'the fine mist in the air' but by this time they were down to sea level and still in chalk. They were conscious of the deep Bevendean Valley to the north and offered the notion that because the valley intercepted the natural water course it prevented water from reaching the bottom of the well. The 'four wise men', as they were called, offered advice which resulted in the Guardians ordering further headings be cut and joined and trial wells be sunk which were ultimately filled in. The eastern chamber looked more promising and it was at the end of this heading that the second shaft was sunk but in the interests of economy only 48inches in diameter.

A local man by the name of Wright (or this could have been Catts who described himself as a Geologist) said that the maximum height of water could be as much as 1700 feet and that the expense of pumping it over to the Brighton Workhouse would be thirty times the supply price from the Water Board. Mr Woolett a Water Board Representative, said the Board was keen to supply a piped service as they were under an agreement to supply Mr Beard's tenants in the vicinity.

A second winch was sanctioned for the lower shaft and work began, but shortly after, a layer of flints were encountered which raised their hopes of finding water. Their hopes were dashed and they again found themselves in chalk and in the most difficult conditions imaginable. Recesses were built into the side of the shaft where men could stand and haul the heavy iron buckets containing wet chalk and heavy engineering bricks as well as cement mortar vertically in both directions. A square yard of dry engineering bricks weighed nearly 500 lbs! Progress was very slow and the danger increased with depth. By the time they reached the 600-foot mark 45 men were working day and night. Clothing offered no protection so men worked naked in appalling conditions, many probably being injured but only one man died. His wife received £6 pounds compensation. Soil conditions changed gradually from grey marl with blue seams to blue marl with grey seams between the 785 and 968-foot level, then they hit greensand, then gault clay which varied in colour from ash brown to black and bluish black. They passed through more clay with seams of green sand with much vegetable matter that would have been millions of years old, layers of wood and pyrites giving off a sulphurous stench then into brown clay not effervescing with acid as the rest of the gault did, but with hard white nodules. As they approached the 1280 foot (390.14m) level they hit greensand with seams of white sand mixed with ancient pebbles but less than a metre further on, red sand where the water was struck.

The construction of the last 300 feet of the well must have been intolerably slow and expensive compared to the upper levels. When Mr Maynard exhibited specimens of the various strata which the workmen had to dig through it gradually dawned on everyone that their task could be hopeless. He produced the very last piece taken out of the well prior to the flow of water and although it had a rather rocky appearance, it was quite green and crumbled into sand when pressed.

The silver medal presented to the well diggers in 1862. Mr Huggett was given a gold medal.

It is well known that the Guardians of the Poor argued about the cost of digging the well which had reached £90 a week and jests in the weekly newspapers were frequent. A lack of confidence by the public in ever finding water and a semi-hostile press made itself known in the town where the ratepayers were angry at being told that the cost had risen to £6,583, far in excess of that predicted. Their patience had almost run out when on the 16th March 1862 the steiner or bricklayer remarked that although he had been sending up soil he had done no steining whatsoever and the floor of the well was no lower. Whether the steiner realized that he had been standing on a thin crust of earth is not known but on the balance of probability I believe he must have done. We must remember the men were not 'professional' well diggers who would have recognized the signs and effect of a piston of gault slowly being raised by the pressure of water below; these were men from the Workhouse in Brighton and quite unused to this work. It was whilst the relief team was making their 45-minute descent down the shafts on that Sunday evening that a terrible noise came from below as water broke through. Three men, Mr Eastwood, Jack Scroggins and Bill Tomkins all claimed to be the last man to leave the floor of the well; however, a report in the Brighton Guardian 1862 which listed the surnames of all the workers attending the celebratory dinner showed Scroggins and Tomkins were not present. It stated that Mr Eastwood was officially honoured as being the last man to leave the 1,285 foot level.

It had taken four years, the loss of one life that we know about and a substantial use of unskilled labour to bring the well into operation. The workforce cannot go unmentioned for it was they who braved those horrendous, miserable, dark and almost airless shafts to work in a tube of brickwork only four feet in diameter twelve hundred feet below the ground. The men, mainly paupers, were not rewarded for the danger they

Mrs Joan Bevington - Henk peers down to the trap door securing the well at the Nuffield Hospital in 2006. Mrs Henk lived in Crescent Drive during the 1920s and occasionally revisits the village.

faced because they were from the Brighton Workhouse and their low or almost negligible wages created the substantial saving in cost for the Guardians and the substantial saving in poor relief. It is thought that being sent for a spell 'On the Warren' was used as a punishment for workhouse misdemeanour. Their reward, such as it was, consisted of a dinner and an inscribed medal to commend their 'Hard work, Patience and Perseverance', likewise Mr Huggett the Workmaster also received a medal but his was in gold. It is not known whether George Maynard, who inherited the role of Surveyor when Samuel North terminated his contract, received a medal or not.

A few years after the well came into use a rather sad tragedy occurred when three boys, who helped William George the engineer every day, took two other boys into the unlocked engine room very early in the morning to ride up and down the well on a timber seat or 'donkey' by candlelight. Two boys were descending when the winch slipped from one boy's hands which broke the safety

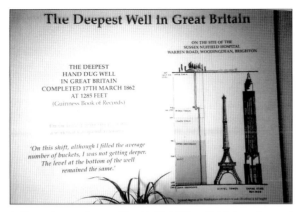

The Deepest Well in Great Britain

ON THE SITE OF THE
SUSSEX NUFFIELD HOSPITAL
WARREN ROAD, WOODINGDEAN, BRIGHTON

THE DEEPEST
HAND DUG WELL
IN GREAT BRITAIN
COMPLETED 17TH MARCH 1862
AT 1285 FEET
(Guinness Book of Records)

'On this shift, although I filled the average
number of buckets, I was not getting deeper.
The level at the bottom of the well
remained the same.'

In the entrance foyer of the Nuffield Hospital this wall mural records 'The Deepest Well in Great Britain' and is taken from THMP. Photo courtesy of Mrs Bevington-Henk.

catch and the two boys plummeted to their deaths. Having hovered over the centre of the well in the bucket of an excavator I can easily imagine the terror in the faces of those poor boys as they fell over 400 feet down the shaft into a few feet of water.

Years later, sometime during the 1950s a man, a stranger, visited Woodingdean from Australia enquiring about the well, the story of which was little known, and was directed it is said to farmer Harold West for help. Harold was shown a medal and was told that the man had inherited it, but as Harold knew nothing of the well or its whereabouts sent him on his way and the medal has never been found.

What was it like down below? The workforce worked day and night and the hours of employment were revised and reflected the degree of difficulty of a person's job and the depth at which they worked. Surface workers were put on a twelve hour day, those at the top of the lower shaft, ten hours, winchmen on upper platforms in the lower shaft eight hours and winchmen on the lower platform in the same shaft six hours. Only one man could work on the well floor and he too worked a six hour shift. There were four steiners who dug and bricked up as they went.

The names of the men who attended the dinner are recorded but there may have been a few that for particular reasons were unable to be there. The Guardians decided that such an achievement deserved a civic reception and engaged the Brighton Workhouse band to lead the men from The Level to the

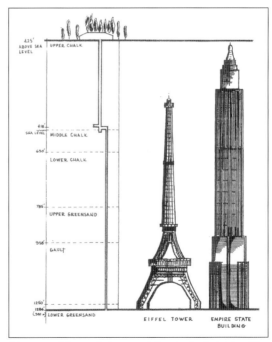

Diagram of the well shown relative to the heights of the Eiffel Tower and the Empire State Building. A mural of this diagram appears in the entrance lobby of the Nuffield Hospital in Warren Road.

Town Hall where tables were set for a 'plain dinner', but at the last minute the weather turned foul and the march was cancelled. However, not to be put off, the men marched holding aloft the tools of their trade, now polished up and sporting streamers and wearing distinctive rosettes with Isaac Huggett wearing a gold-lettered sash. The men entered the Town Hall to great applause and passed under the Royal Standard and Union Jack to take their places at the long tables to await the speeches and presentation of medals. Formality was forgotten and Guardians and officials intermixed with the men. At intervals around the tables there stood a bottle of water which had cost so much to find.

The following workers are listed as attending the Celebratory Dinner - Bond, Clapsom, J Davey, Devonish, Eastwood, Ede, Elliot, Falls, Pugdon, Foord, J Foord, Foster, Frost, Goldsmith, Harris, Hammond, Harlott, Hillman, Horne, I Huggett, Ireland, D Juden, H Juden, Leney, Markwick, Martin, Mitchell, Morrison, Mowbrey, Painter, Parsons, Penfold, Pettett, Pettett, Pettett, Pierce, Pocket, Russells, Simmonds, C Sallis, H Sallis, Satcher, G Satcher, H Smith, J Smith, Stephens, Tigwell, Towner, Towner, G Towner, Trangmar, W Vine, Wait, H Wilson, Winder, Williams.

It is known that some of the workers were married but one can only assume that in the interest of economy none of the wives were invited to attend the dinner.

As an interesting footnote George Maynard's first grandson, Magnus Volk, wrote to the Director of the Geological Survey Museum on the 5th March 1934 with details of the well. At the time of writing Magnus was 83 years old. See THMP page 235 for a copy of the letter.

◄○►◄○►◄○►

Standean Bottom where cricket was played in the mid-18th Century. In the 1750s cricket was played on 'Basden Flats' between teams from Rottingdean, Lewes and Brighthelmstone. Leading exponents were Thomas Clare, landlord of the White Horse and King of Prussia of Rottingdean, and Thomas Goldsmith, landlord of the Wheatsheaf at Lewes, an old sporting house. In 1758 an account in 'Brighton in the Golden Times' (1880) refers to a cricket match to be held on the 28th June will be play'd at Rottingdean near Lewes for a guinea a man; Newick, Chailey, Lindfield and Hamsey against Lewes, Brighthelmstone and Rottingdean whose players were John Newington, Stenning Beard, Thomas Clare and Phillip Emery. Not only did landlord Clare play cricket but in May 1758 he advertised to acquaint the public with bull-baiting at his inn in Rottingdean, he also advertised for persons to bring their cocks to fight at five shillings a battle - 'A good Twelvepenny Ordinary at One o'clock.' Rottingdean at the period must have been a lively place! (See cricket THMP pages 252-253)

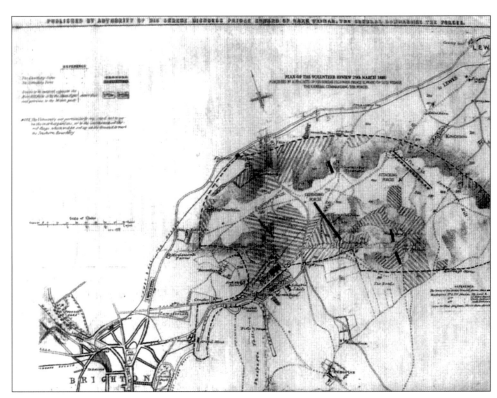

The Volunteers' Review of 1880 took place over an area from Sheepcote Valley to Kingston village. It was over this area of the Downs that in 1797 a mock battle was commanded by General Sir Charles Grey, attended by the Prince of Wales when living in Brighton. A water spout put paid to one 'battle' putting the men to rout. In 1810 ten thousand troops took part in a military review with an estimated 30,000 spectators looking on. In 1942 the British Army occupied this valley for a more deadly game of war that was to leave the village of Balsdean decimated and lost forever. Picture courtesy of Peter Longstaff-Tyrrell

Balsdean, the lost village in pictures

The early history of Balsdean is told in Chapter 7 of THMP and in Peter Longstaff-Tyrrell's book 'Lost Villages of East Sussex'.

The rear of Balsdean Manor House during the mid-1920s with Ben, Phoebe and Les Edwards seated by the wall. The house was built to replace the original house burned down in 1764.

The front of the Georgian Manor House about the same time. The Woodman family were the last family to occupy the house in 1942 when they were given two weeks to quit by the Military Authorities. For the history of the Woodman family see THMP pages 127-133. According to Peter Longstaff -Tyrrell in his book 'Lost Villages of East Sussex' the Brighton Corporation sought £55,726 compensation for the loss of Balsdean but ultimately settled on £8,433 with the Land Agency.

A further view of the lovely old Manor House. Mr Woodman once told me that the house was so cold

in winter that the draught would lift the carpets off the floor. In some respects the Woodmans were pleased to leave in 1942 and make their way to Exebridge in Somerset where they remained for five years before moving on to Blakes Farm also in Somerset where they farmed over 1000 acres until 1985. Norah Woodman died in 1961 and her husband Guy passed away in 1972. Their son Gerald retired from farming in 1985 but would often revisit Balsdean over the years. I had the pleasure of meeting him on one such occasion and listening to his very unique story of life in a downland manor farmhouse.

A lovely pastoral view of the Manor House and vegetable garden neatly ploughed and ready for sowing. Cows graze infront of the house which masks the chapel. The pair of farm workers' cottages peeps out above the largest of the trees and Norton Farm and the barns lay under Castle Hill before it became a National Nature Reserve. A Saxon warrior lies watchfully at peace on the summit.

A similar view in the summer of 1942 but by this time the farm had been ringed with barbed wire and was desolate, devoid of workers and livestock and two Churchill tanks on the roadway look to the start of razing the chapel, houses and barns to the ground.

The flint barn, formerly the Chapel, built around 1138 and used as a place of worship until 1580 when the vicar of Rottingdean visited the chapel four times a year. The photograph clearly shows where the chancel once stood but no east chancel wall was ever found. The end wall, formerly with narrow arched opening between nave and chancel, was added later to make it more suitable as a stable. A stone plaque in the grass shows where once the chapel stood. For details of the chapel and a brief history of Balsdean see THMP 'Balsdean' Chapter 7.

The early Norman chapel in 1927. Long deconsecrated and recently re-roofed the 800-year-old building is now used as a barn. On this side of the barn three burials were discovered, two children aged about five and six and one adult, probably a man aged about forty. From their condition it is probable that the burials were of medieval date. The pair of farm workers' cottages are to the right and Norton Farm House beyond under Castle Hill.

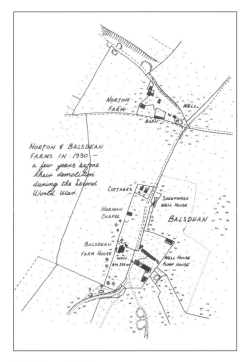

Balsdean, 1930.

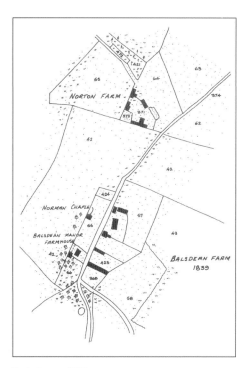

Balsdean, 1839

Norton Farmhouse and barn under Castle Hill in 1927. On the hillside behind the cottage were planted fruit trees which still bear fruit to this day. John Munro lived in this cottage with his uncle and aunt, Jack and May Nicholls during the 1930s.

A much earlier photograph of Norton Farmhouse, barn and dilapidated fence, a product of tenant farming when income was low and they worked long and unsociable hours. No running water, electricity, gas or proper drainage was available at the time. Lighting was by oil lamps and sanitation primitive. This building was not the original farmhouse. In the 1820s Norton Farm was purchased by William Ridge and from 1825 the original farmhouse was used by Dr King, son-in-law of Dr Hooker, the Vicar of Rottingdean, and Mr William Attree, as a lunatic asylum for twenty patients 'for the recovery of persons afflicted with mental alienation'. When the Brighton authorities removed their lunatic patients from Bethnal Green in 1827 they were sent to Norton Farm but in1829 were moved on to a licensed asylum at Ringmer, most probably because Norton was unlicensed, isolated and in a primitive condition. In March 1827 Sir W Scott Bart reported -

'I have this day visited Balsdean and am perfectly satisfied with that cleanly and comfortable state in which I found patients. The house appears perfectly clean and sufficiently secure. I have the belts and straps for restraining refractory patients and consider them as little inconvenient to the wearer as possible.

William Attree joined the Ordnance Medical Department as 2nd Assistant Surgeon on August 1806, becoming 1st Assistant surgeon on 6th January 1809. He retired in 1819 and resided, and perhaps practised, in Brighton and afterwards at Sudbury near Harrow where he died in 1846. William was a member of the prominent Attree family of lawyers in Brighton and is mentioned as being Surgeon to the King.

It has been suggested that the patients were held in the loft of Balsdean Manor House but I find that difficult to believe since twenty patients plus the staff could not possibly have been housed there,

besides which the manor was owned by wealthy Joseph Montifiore and occupied by a yeoman farmer William Ridge at the time.

The remains of Norton Barn destroyed during the war and before the army returned to demolish and bury the debris in the late 1940s.

The only remains of Norton Farmhouse or Barn.

Farm workers' cottages built about the turn of the 20th century. Workers would have been glad to have fine houses as these. Only a mound of grass now provides the clue as to where the cottages once stood. Picture from the 1920s.

The remains of a Myers Bulldozer Power Working Head imported from Ashland, Ohio probably about 1925 as it is similar to one on the well at Norton Farm sunk by Dando in 1922. Norton well yielded 700 gallons an hour with water standing at 62 feet. See THMP Page 260. Note the bullet hole.

The quiet valley almost opposite Balsdean Manor House where sheep may safely graze. Traces of the old farm buildings can still be found in the grass. The tree is reputed to mark the spot where cellars used by smugglers once stashed their illicit contraband.

A poignant photograph of the farms immediately after the war when people were again allowed to walk there. The chapel has disappeared into a heap of rubble which is my first memory of the place. The two cottages are standing but the roof tiles are partially gone as have the barns in the foreground and much of Norton Farm. Although the Manor House is not seen here it had been entirely demolished and lay as a pile of rubble behind the trees. The situation remained for a considerable time until the Army returned with bulldozers and finally demolished and buried the remains and cleared the land of munitions. Even today, the odd bullet and small pieces of bombs can still be found in the grass and among the undergrowth.

The remains of Balsdean after the war with most of the rubble gone. The hill opposite is heavily pockmarked with shell holes, some of which are discernible today. Around to the left and out of sight there stood a WWII moving gun carriage and target in the form of a figure of eight. That now has entirely disappeared.

Gerald Woodman stands among the bushes near to Norton Farm where during the war he and his father Guy Woodman buried supplies of marmalade, paraffin and blankets, hidden there in case of an emergency or an enemy landing. The Woodman family lived in the Manor House from 1924 to 1942 when they were evacuated to the West Country, leaving several tons of coal in the cellar and their beloved grand piano in the lounge. Gerald attended the Rottingdean Primary School on a pony which he stabled in the village and then Brighton College which he didn't care for preferring to be at home on the Downs which he so loved. I had the pleasure of meeting Gerald on his last visit to Balsdean.

Barrie Smith inspects the outline of the foundations of the two farm workers' cottages near the chapel in September 2002. Climatic conditions occasionally reveal the outline in the soil.

The only remains of the 245-year-old Manor House in the grass.

A group of 'students' of local history sit on the remains of the Manor House wall in 2006. Pat and Len Norris are far left, Lynda Wymark sits fifth from the right in a red top and the author is in the middle in a green shirt.

INDEX

Squires, Captain 114.
St John Baptist School 152.
St Margaret's Church, Rottingdean 23 93
    146.
St Mary's Home 113.
St Wulfram Church 21 23 24.
Stevens George 143.
Stowell, Albert 55 68 99 100 101 127.
Stowell, Alvida 100 110.
Subsidy Rolls 18 19 20.

T
Thrower & Woolgar 89 123 124.
Thistle Cake Shop 141.
Tilling, Thomas 62 86 90 92 96 102
Titchenor, Mr 88-90.
Todd, Wally 143.
Tolman, Arthur 23.
Tullett, Kate and May 61 67.

V.
Van Der Elst, Violet Annie 64.
Vanderborght, Roger 64.
Villata de Rottygeden 20.
Volk, Magnus 146 158.

W.
Wadere, Rob le 19.
Waleby, Philip de 18.
Walesbone, Hundreda 19.
Walton, PC, Jack 142.
Ward, Mr (Architect) 123.
Wardean Brow 83.
Warenne, Earl de 20.
Warr, Mr 44 53.
Warren Farm 21 25 27 28 148.
Warren Farm Dairy Farm 18 26.
Warren Farm House 14.
Warren Farm Industrial School 24 26 32
    88 95 121 146 147 149.
Warren Farm Road 146 148.
Warren Plantation 33 147.
Warren Stores, the 19.
Weike, Le (1611) 16 27.
Weik Lez 27.
Welesmere 17.
Well, names of workers 158.

Well, The 152-158.
Wells, Mr (bandleader) 147.
Wesleyan Methodist Chapel 24.
West, Albert 89.
West, Colin and Margaret 50.
West family names 52.
West, Harold and Peggy. 51 134 157.
Whitfield & Co 64.
Whittaker, Mr 53 54.
Whittle, Rev Arthur 116.
Wick Avenue 38.
Wick Barn 20 39 117.
Wick Bottom (1714) 14 15 17 27 28.
Wick Farm 14 25 27 28 55 65.
Wick Farm Cottage 89.
Wick Farm Lodge 37.
Wick Laine 28.
Wick or Wyke Estate 13 16 17 83 84 86
    90 91 94.
Wickhovel 17.
Will le Sopere 19.
Willard, William 51.
Williams, Rev ML 120.
Wintle, Leslie and Shirley 19.
Woodendean 81 82.
WoodenDean 81.
Wood-en-dean 82.
Woodendean Farm 15 25 28 59 64 68 81
    82 92.
Wooden-dean Farm 81 89.
Woodendene 82.
Woodendon Farm 81.
Wooderdean 81.
Woodingcote 81.
Woodingdean Church Choir (1940s) 116.
Woodingdean Community Assn 32 56.
Woodingdean Copse 83.
Woodingdean Farm 28 64.
Woodingdean Football Club 55 77 100
    132 142.
Woodingdean House 59 64 81 82 84 88.
Woodingdean Laine 83.
Woodingdean Road 29 93.
Woodingdean Temporary Council School
    No 42 97 115 131 149.
Woodingdean Ward 86 94 95 96 98.
Woodland Grange 82.

Woodman, Guy, Nora and Gerald 161
    167.
Woods, Mrs. "Australia" 103.
Woolgar, Sam 23 55.
Wootingde(a)n 81 82.
Wymark, Lynda, Jack, Alan, Brian and
    Elaine 55 131.

Y.

Yeatman, Chris, Walter, Miriam and
    Rhoda 104 105 109.
Younsmere 17.